PEOPLE OF THE DAY 4

by
Peter Wynter Bee

Illustrated by
Lucy

© People of the Day Limited, 2009
Sunnymede, New England Hill, West End, Woking, Surrey GU24 9PY
Tel: 01276 859483

Text by: Peter F Wynter Bee
Illustrated by: Lucy

A CIP catalogue record of this book is available from the British Library.

ISBN 13: 978-0-9548110-3-7

Published by People of the Day Limited
Printed and bound in Great Britain by Taurus Media

Charity Supported

People of the Day is sold to raise funds for:

The Cystic Fibrosis Trust

Cystic Fibrosis (CF) is the UK's most common life-threatening inherited disease, affecting over 8,000 people in the UK alone. It is caused by a single faulty gene that controls the movement of salt in the body.

Around 1 in 25 people in the UK carry the faulty gene - that's over two million people. Each week five babies are born with CF and three young lives are lost to CF.

CF affects a number of internal organs, especially the lungs and digestive system, by clogging them with a thick sticky mucus resulting in infections and inflammation which make it hard to breathe and digest food.

THERE IS CURRENTLY NO CURE FOR CYSTIC FIBROSIS

The CF Trust is the major funder of medical and scientific CF research in the UK. Currently it spends around £4 million annually on research to find an effective treatment for CF through gene therapy, which it is thought will provide the nearest thing to a cure in the foreseeable future. The CF Trust has brought together the UK's leading CF geneticists to form the UK CF Gene Therapy Consortium. The scientists are based in Edinburgh, London and Oxford. The CF Trust has pledged to raise the necessary funds to carry out this work and so far it has invested well over £15 million in this project.

A further £800,000 is spent each year on research aimed at other aspects of CF, such as infection, inflammation, drug therapy and the pancreas.

Through research, better understanding and treatment of CF, life expectancy is increasing. When the CF Trust was founded in 1964, life expectancy was just five years. Until recently it was 31, it now stands at 35 – not good enough but getting better.

The Trust supports specialist trained CF nurses and physiotherapists who can help CF patients live at home. It can lend CF patients specialised equipment and it also provides support for the families of CF sufferers, including financial assistance where appropriate.

Thanks to Taurus Media Services Limited who have sponsored Volume 4

Foreword

Thank you for purchasing this, the fourth volume of 'People of the Day'. You, or whoever had the excellent idea of buying it for you, have just helped fund the work of the Cystic Fibrosis Trust.

When I started publishing 'People of the Day', four years ago, the average life expectancy for someone born with Cystic Fibrosis was 31 years, today it's 35, but when my sister, Annie, was born in 1962 it was just 3 years. Many sufferers now live into their 40s and 50s (Annie actually died in 2007, aged 44) but so many still die as children, teenagers or young adults.

The profits from the sales of 'People of the Day' and the limited edition caricature prints all go to the Cystic Fibrosis Trust.

With Volume 4 of 'People of the Day' we continue to profile 52 'People of the Day', aiming to celebrate their achievements, demonstrate what was often a difficult path to success, chart the obstacles overcome and inspire others to achieve their own personal goals. Forget the tittle-tattle and muck raking; the real stories are so much more interesting.

In the following pages you will find those who have left us awestruck and inspired by sporting prowess made to look easy but achieved through great effort and determination, entrepreneurs who never took "No" for an answer, and people who simply enriched our lives by their talents and actions – as we go to press Alfred Brendel, Joanna Lumley and Ranulph Fiennes spring to mind.

Since we normally only write up those who are still with us, keeping up to date is a challenge, but nothing compared to Ranulph Fiennes's challenge of reaching the summit of Everest as the first British pensioner to do so. With only days before POD4 went to print we had a quick addition to his profile!

The Cutting Room Floor

We are limited to 650 words per profile – a source of endless frustration as we are forced to cut items we would love to include. So we have decided to share the following gems we had to omit.

The 'Today' presenter, John Timpson, was thrilled to learn that the nuns at Libby Purves's convent school had ruled that radios could not be taken into the bathroom as they felt his manly tones were inappropriate in an environment where young girls were undressing.

Aged 21, Cilla Black was invited to perform in 'The Royal Variety Show' and all her family came down to watch. The next day they confessed they'd been so overawed by their proximity to The Queen that they'd spent the whole evening watching her instead of Cilla.

John Sentamu frequently quoted his mother "Don't point your finger because the other three are pointing back at you."

He also spoke of when he came to God, aged 10, and felt moved to confess to his father that he had stolen books to buy banana pancakes; as a result, his father caned him in front of the whole school – a pastoral practice he assured his interviewer he did not follow with his own parishioners.

We were amused to find that according to Felix Dennis's ten levels of wealth (up to The Super Rich – who are richer than The Filthy Rich) we might hope one day to qualify as The Comfortable Poor.

Having written to those we include in POD, and sent them their caricature and a draft profile for comments and amendments, sometimes we come into the office to find a message on the answerphone from the recipient. With some trepidation we call back, what is going to be the reaction? Kate Hoey was charming but most insistent that she could not be portrayed wearing trousers as she and Betty Boothroyd had taken a decision many years ago always to wear skirts when working.

As the website attracts more and more hits we found a plaintive cry clearly aimed at Delia "I am unable to find Delia Smith's frozen flan cases small for strawberry tartlets - Sainsburys have stopped stocking them please will you let me know where I can get them."

We have really enjoyed putting together volume 4 and thank all those who took the trouble to write back with helpful comments and kind words.

Please spread the word about 'People of the Day' – it really can make a difference fund raising for the CF Trust, and who knows what difference it could make when it inspires someone to have just one more push at going that extra mile to achieve the dream they thought might be out of reach.

I am definitely not the cook in our family but, ever optimistic, I hope that one day I shall be inspired to be the one the children telephone for advice when they are halfway through preparing dinner for friends. With this in mind I now have Limited Edition Prints of the caricatures of Delia Smith, Nigella Lawson and Gordon Ramsay (if you're feeling brave!) on my kitchen wall, which can be purchased through our website www.peopleoftheday.com to inspire you in your kitchen.

Finally, this volume is dedicated to my sister, Annie, and the families of all those born with Cystic Fibrosis. There are many individual examples of fantastic fund raising efforts – sometimes one off amazing stunts and sometimes just plugging away for years with Christmas sales, organising events and rattling tins. My mother, Peggy Wynter Bee, has been involved with the CF Trust since it was set up and, aged 84, she still organises her area's annual CF week. Despite being registered disabled she will be found with her collecting tin shaming us all by her energy and the amount she manages to collect. As she said to the Chief Executive of the CF Trust, Rosie Barnes, the last time she saw her "Make sure you find the cure before I'm gone".

Contents

HRH The Prince of Wales KG KT GCB OM

' "I'd rather be criticised for doing things rather than not doing them." '

He has been Prince of Wales for over 50 years. An undefined role that could simply consist of uncontroversial ribbon cutting and ceremonial duties, this has never been Prince Charles's vision. Whilst remaining strictly non partisan, he will question government policy and raise unfashionable areas of concern – as a Cambridge undergraduate, in a Union debate, he highlighted pollution, not a major issue then, and the dangers of humans becoming creatures of technology.

He was born on 14th November 1948 at Buckingham Palace. When his mother became Queen, Charles, aged 3, became heir apparent and Duke of Cornwall, Duke of Rothesay, Earl of Carrick, Baron Renfrew, Lord of the Isles and Prince and Great Steward of Scotland. Aged 5 he made his first official foreign visit, to Malta, on Britannia's maiden voyage.

A governess was engaged for his primary education but, unlike previous royal heirs, he was then sent to school starting at Hill House, London. In 1957 he transferred to Cheam, a boarding school and, aged 9, was created Prince of Wales and Earl of Chester. His holidays were spent at Balmoral and Sandringham where his love of the countryside and interest in environmental matters developed.

In 1962 he went to Gordonstoun, Scotland, where he suffered acute homesickness, but enjoyed art, sports, history and music, and was appointed School Guardian (Head Boy). In 1966 he spent two terms in Australia at Timbertop, part of Geelong Grammar School. Whilst there he went on a school trip to Papua New Guinea, afterwards writing an essay expressing concern that the traditions of the Papuan people were being lost – a theme he later developed.

He became the first heir apparent to take GCE 'O' and 'A' Levels, before attending Trinity College, Cambridge where he read Anthropology and Archaeology, and History. At school he had enjoyed amateur dramatics, where his shyness disappeared, and at Trinity he joined the College's drama group, appearing in two of its annual revues. In 1969 he spent a term at the University College of Wales at Aberystwyth studying Welsh and the Principality's history, prior to his investiture at Caernarfon Castle. During these years he also attended Privy Council meetings, travelled on state visits and took his seat in the House of Lords, as well as becoming a Counsellor of State and Knight of the Garter.

In 1971 he joined the RAF, training as a jet pilot, having previously gained his private pilot's licence. Later that year he embarked on his Naval career, qualifying as a helicopter pilot and commanding HMS Bronington. He currently holds the ranks of Admiral in the Royal Navy, Air Chief Marshal in the RAF and General in the Army.

On 29th July 1981 he married the Lady Diana Spencer and she became HRH The Princess of Wales; they had two sons, Prince William and Prince Harry. The marriage was dissolved in 1996. A year later Diana, Princess of Wales died in a car crash in Paris. Prince Charles flew to Paris with her sisters to bring her body back to London. He accompanied their two sons, then aged 15 and 12, as they walked behind her coffin to Westminster Abbey, past huge crowds. In 2005 he married Camilla Parker Bowles who became HRH The Duchess of Cornwall.

Today, the Prince has three main areas of work: 'Supporting The Queen', 'The Prince's Charities' and 'Promoting and Protecting'. The first is self-explanatory. The second is a grouping of 20 'not for profit' organisations of which the Prince is either Patron or President, and the third includes ensuring that the views of all, but particularly those who might not otherwise be represented, are heard – the need to recognise the human dimension. His work for charity raises over £119 million annually and the Prince has done a tremendous amount to assist young people towards a better future. His involvement in another 400 organisations reflects his concerns and interests – not least putting the 'Great' back into Britain.

HM King Abdullah II lbn Al Hussein
'King of Jordan'

The 43rd generation direct descendant of the Prophet Mohammad, Peace Be Upon Him, His Majesty King Abdullah II became monarch on 7 February 1999. Like his father, the late King Hussein, King Abdullah has made the welfare of Jordan's people the cornerstone of his policies for national development, regional peace and global coexistence. His special concern for the future of Jordan's youth emphasises engagement, education and opportunity. He has paired economic reforms with political liberalisation and innovative national development, overseen sweeping educational reforms and energised Jordan's private sector.

To alleviate Jordan's pressing economic needs King Abdullah ushered in structural reform and modernisation, integration with world economies, and globalisation. He has brought together public and private sectors – domestic and global – through large joint initiatives to meet the challenges of job creation, opportunity for Jordan's young and the alleviation of poverty. He championed Jordan's accession to the WTO, presided over Jordan becoming the first Arab country to sign a free trade agreement with the US, and built international economic alliances.

Diplomatically he has been the voice of Jordan's progressive policies expanding global justice and cooperation. Taking up the Hashemite family's historic role, he champions the rights, achievements and values of Muslims worldwide. In 2004, he worked with Islamic scholars to release the Amman Message, reaching a global audience with Islam's guiding principles of peace, tolerance and dialogue among faiths. In his father's footsteps, King Abdullah renewed a commitment to peace in the region on the basis of the two-state solution and establishment of a viable, independent and geographically contiguous Palestinian state with East Jerusalem as its capital, living in peace alongside Israel, in accordance with UN resolutions and the 2002 Arab Peace Initiative.

The eldest son of His Majesty King Hussein bin Talal (1935-1999) and HRH Princess Muna Al Hussein, he was born in Amman on 30 January 1962 and named Abdullah for his great grandfather, founder of modern Jordan. Educated at the Islamic Educational College, Amman, he later attended St Edmund's School, UK and Deerfield Academy, US. He then attended Pembroke College, Oxford, and Georgetown University.

In 1980 he enrolled at Sandhurst, and served in the British Army as a Reconnaissance Troop Leader in the UK and Germany. In 1985, he returned to Jordan to serve in the Armed Forces (Armoured Corps, 3rd Division). Rising through the ranks to lieutenant-colonel, he attended military courses in Jordan and the UK, served on attachment to the Special Forces and qualified as a Cobra attack helicopter pilot. After service as Commander of the 2nd Armoured Battalion, 40th Armoured Brigade, he was named Deputy Commander, Jordanian Special Forces, becoming Commander in 1993. In 1996, he re-organised the special forces and elite units into Special Operations Command (SOCOM). In 1998, as SOCOM Commander, he was promoted Major General.

Off-duty the Prince loved land, sea, and air sports, including parachuting and became a Jordan National Rally champion. He continues to enjoy aquatic sports. King Abdullah has an interest in ancient weapons, and maintains a world-class collection of military artefacts. His army service was a source of personal pride, and he has great respect for those who serve, describing Jordan's armed forces as the "foremost symbol of honour, bravery, sacrifice and belonging." During army service he was often dispatched on official diplomatic and military missions, serving as regent in King Hussein's absence. In 1993 Prince Abdullah met the beautiful Rania Al-Yassin, daughter of a family with Palestinian origins. Within six months they were married and now have four children, Prince Hussein, Princess Iman, Princess Salma and Prince Hashem.

The Rt Hon Helen Clark
'Former New Zealand Prime Minister'

She served as the 37th Prime Minister of New Zealand and was the second female to hold that office and the first to have won office at an election. She led the country in a Labour government from 1999 until 2008.

Helen Elizabeth Clark was born in Hamilton on 26 February 1950, the eldest of four daughters of George and Margaret Clark, staunch National Party supporters, which led to heated arguments with her father on her visits home. Her father ran the family farm in Te Pahu whilst her mother worked as a primary school teacher.

She was educated at Te Pahu Primary School and later boarded at Epsom Girls' Grammar School in Auckland. In 1968 she went to the University of Auckland where she studied History, German, English and Political Studies, graduating in 1974 with an MA (Hons).

In 1971 she joined the Labour Party after becoming actively involved in politics while studying at university and thereafter became a lecturer in political studies. She stood for Parliament for the first time in the National safe seat of Piako in 1975 but naturally was unsuccessful.

In 1981 she was one of four women to enter Parliament and was elected as MP for Mt Albert. At that time her party was committed to free-market policies, a line she was not willing to follow saying "If the market is left to sort matters out, social injustice will be heightened and suffering in the community will grow with the neglect the market fosters."

During her first four year term she became a member of the Statutes Revision Committee and in her second term she chaired the Select Committee on Foreign Affairs and the Select Committee on Disarmament and Arms Control. In 1987 she became a Cabinet Minister responsible for Housing and Conservation. In 1989 she became the Minister of Health and in August of that year became the Minister of Labour and Deputy Prime Minister.

She chaired and was a member of numerous committees and in 1990 she became Deputy Leader of the Opposition, Opposition Spokesperson for Health and Labour and a member of the Social Services Select Committee and Labour Select Committee. She became Leader of the Opposition in 1993 after a successful challenge for the leadership of the parliamentary Labour Party.

She was elected as Prime Minister in 1999 also becoming Minister for Arts, Culture and Heritage and, at the same time, had ministerial responsibility for the NZ Security Intelligence Service and for Ministerial Services. The Labour Party lost the election in November 2008 and she resigned as leader. In 2009 she was named Administrator of the UN Development Program.

She is a supporter of New Zealand becoming a Republic and throughout her time in office has backed the abolition of appeals to the Privy Council, the setting up of the Supreme Court of NZ, the abolition of the honours system and the abolition of the title "Queen's Counsel". There have also been changes such as the introduction of child tax credits, a change in industrial-relations law and several increases to the minimum wage, changes in tertiary-education financing with the abolition of student loans, legal provision for civil unions, introduction of 14 weeks parental leave and the Property (Relationships) Act.

In 2008 she won the United Nations Environment Programme Champions of the Earth award in recognition of the Government's promotion of sustainability initiatives. She is an Honorary Member of the International Raoul Wallenberg Foundation, a keen concert goer and opera lover. She regularly visits the gym to keep fit and loves hiking and cross-country skiing. In 1999 she successfully climbed Mt Kilimanjaro. She married Dr Peter Davis in 1981.

Michael Gove MP
'The Tories' One-Man-Think-Tank'

As Shadow Secretary for Children, Schools and Families Michael is passionate about ensuring that children from disadvantaged backgrounds are not let down by the school system. As he has said, he could all too easily have been one of them.

Born in Edinburgh in 1967 he was adopted when he was four months old by a family in Aberdeen, which is where he grew up. His father ran a fish processing business and his mother was a lab assistant at Aberdeen University prior to working at Aberdeen School for the Deaf. They worked hard and made sacrifices to give Michael the best education they could, both at a state school as well as at the fee paying Robert Gordon's College. His sister, who is also adopted, is deaf and Michael learned sign language to communicate with her.

He read English at Lady Margaret Hall, Oxford and became President of the Union. After university he went into journalism, working for local and national newspapers, radio and TV, including R4's 'Today' programme. In 1996 he joined The Times where, for nearly a decade, he was a leader writer and senior editor. Whilst at The Times he worked with Frances Lawrence, wife of murdered headmaster, Philip Lawrence, to set up the Anti-Street Crime Campaign which established awards for good citizenship among youngsters, and influenced legislation to ban combat knives.

Only a year apart from David Cameron at Oxford the two did not immediately become close. However, twenty years on Michael is one of Cameron's top advisors. It was David Cameron who persuaded him to stand for Parliament in the 2005 election, taking the safe Tory seat of Surrey Heath with a majority of nearly 11,000. In turn Gove persuaded Cameron to stand for Leader of the Conservative Party, "When the issue of the leadership came up, well I'd only been an MP for about, you know, five seconds so it was immensely presumptuous. But I thought there needed to be a modernising candidate. And I thought David was the right person."

He is highly articulate and is a former Chairman of Policy Exchange, a centre-right-think-tank, appropriate for someone William Rees-Mogg dubbed the 'Tories One-Man-Think-Tank'. His books include a biography of Michael Portillo; 'The Price of Peace' about the Northern Ireland peace process, which won the Charles Douglas-Home Prize; and 'Celsius 7/7' in which he warns starkly of the dangers of Islamism and Western appeasement. He has been a member of the R4 'Moral Maze' panel and often appears on 'Any Questions' and 'Newsnight Review'.

His first appointment was as Shadow Minister for Housing & Planning. He clearly relishes his latest front bench role in education saying "Essentially I see my job as acting as a campaigner for the best in state education and trying to improve schools for everyone." This has included trying his hand at teaching. He serves on both the Iraq and the Israel (Vice Chair) All Party Parliamentary Groups as well as others including those for Human Rights, Corporate Responsibility, Housing, Care & Support, and Marine Wildlife; he is a member of the EU Scrutiny Committee. His voting record shows him voting for an investigation into the Iraq War, gay rights and replacing Trident; and against introducing a smoking ban and ID cards.

He continues to write for The Times and his weekly 'Notebook' column is a wonderful cocktail of topical commentary, reviews and excellent diatribes (see 'Blackberry fools' 26.01.09), shaken, not stirred, with witty observations, as in his recent plea for a new CAMRA – Campaign for Real Aperitifs - or as he put it "The terrible metropolitan habit of offering chilled white wine as the first drink of the evening has, like the grey squirrel, spread almost everywhere."

His is married to The Times leader writer, Sarah Vine, and they have two children, a daughter and a son.

Kate Hoey MP
'Free-thinking Labour MP'

Catharine Letitia Hoey was born on 21 June 1946 in County Antrim, Northern Ireland, one of three children to Thomas and Letitia. She was born in a caul (ie, with the amniotic sac or membranes still intact around her as she emerged into the world). Many people regard this as extremely lucky, and it is said that such babies are blessed and go through life with the potential for greatness.

The family owned a small farm where she says she had an idyllic childhood, spent helping out, feeding the pigs and chickens, climbing trees, fishing and riding the family horse. The farm is now run by her brother, on organic principles.

She was educated at Lylehill Primary School and Belfast Royal Academy before going on to the Ulster College of Physical Education, gaining a Diploma in PE. She relocated to England and attended the City of London College where she graduated with a degree in economics. During her student days she was elected Vice-President of the National Union of Students.

She has always had a passion for sport, particularly football and cricket (she is an honorary Vice-President of Surrey County Cricket Club which is in her constituency) and in 1966 was the Northern Ireland High Jump Champion.

Between 1972 and 1976 she lectured at Southwark College and then, between 1976 and 1985, was a Senior Lecturer at Kingsway College. Between 1985 and 1989 she worked for several London football clubs, including Arsenal, Spurs, QPR, Chelsea and Brentford, as Educational Advisor.

In 1989 she won the Vauxhall by-election for the Labour Party. She is a courageous, fiercely independent MP with a strong social conscience. From a rural background (she can still farrow pigs and milk cows) she is unusual amongst Labour MPs in having a real understanding of country matters, and she is well known for her fight against the ban on fox hunting. Since 2005 she has been Chairman of the Countryside Alliance, which has its HQ in her constituency. Keen to introduce inner-city children to Britain's rural world she has organised visits to farms as well as events such as clay pigeon shooting days (after one such day a participant reputedly asked if they could come back another time to shoot some "peasants"). She is Honorary President of both the Clay Pigeon Shooting Association and the British Pistol Club.

In 1997 she became PPS to Frank Field, the Minister for Welfare Reform, a post she held until 1998 when she became Parliamentary Under-Secretary of State at the Home Office. In 1999 she was the UK's first female Sports Minister, a post she held until 2001 when she lost her job for speaking out about the way football handled its finances and criticising the power of the football lobby. She returned to the backbenches where she remains today, promoting the views and interests of her constituents.

She has a keen interest in foreign affairs; she visited Sarajevo when it was under siege, monitored Angola's first democratic elections and travelled undercover to Zimbabwe (2003, 2005 and 2006). Other areas of particular interest include keeping the Royal Mail in public ownership and preserving Post Offices, and provision for pensioners. She has voted against top-up tuition fees, foundation trust hospitals, the Iraq war, ID cards, extended detention without trial and the congestion charge (which cut her constituency in two). In May 2008 she became an unpaid advisor to the Mayor of London, Boris Johnson, as Commissioner for Sport.

She is a Trustee of the Outward Bound Trust, and Vice President of the Great Britain Wheelchair Basketball Association. She passed her driving test at 17 using the family's Mini Clubman, and has remained loyal to Minis ever since, having owned three of them, including the 40th anniversary version.

President Barack Obama
'Change only happens from the top'

The first African American to become a major party's candidate for President of the USA, he is now America's first black President, and its fourth youngest.

Barack Hussein Obama Jnr was born in Honolulu, Hawaii on 4 August 1961. His mother, Ann Dunham, was a white American who had grown up in Kansas. His father, Barack Obama Snr, was a black Kenyan who had won a scholarship to attend university in the States where he met Ann at the University of Manoa, Hawaii. They married in 1960 (marriage between blacks and whites was still regarded as a felony in many parts of the USA then) and Barack Obama Jnr was born the following year. When he was two his parents separated and he only saw his father once again before he died in 1982.

His mother remarried, an Indonesian, with whom she had a daughter, and between the ages of 6 and 10 Obama was brought up in Indonesia. Unable to afford the fees for Jakarta's International school his mother would go into his room at 4am, force-feed him breakfast and then give three hours of English tuition before he went to the local school. She later separated from her second husband and Obama returned to Hawaii to live with his maternal grandparents. He attended the prestigious Punahou School, graduating with honours in 1979, before moving to LA to attend Occidental College, transferring to Columbia University, NY and graduating in 1983 with a degree in political science.

He worked at the Business International Corporation and then the New York Public Interest Relations Group but, in 1985, resigned and moved to Chicago to become a community worker. After three years he realised that getting things changed is easier from the top so he entered Harvard Law School. While studying he worked as an associate for Sidley & Austin, where he met his wife. In February 1990 he became the first African-American Editor of the Harvard Law Review. He graduated magna cum laude in 1991,

and returned to Chicago to practice as a civil rights lawyer. Between 1996 and 2004 he was a Lecturer at the University of Chicago Law School.

His work led him to run for Illinois State Senator, being elected in 1997, and in 2004 he became only the third African American ever to be elected to the US Senate. In 2005 Time magazine named him one of the 100 most influential people; in 2008 he won the Democrat presidential nomination. His legislative record has favoured working families, ethical reforms for government, public education, health care, economic growth, jobs and ending the Iraq War.

His autobiography was published in 1995, 'Dreams From My Father: A Story of Race and Inheritance'; the audio book version won a Grammy award. His second book, 'The Audacity of Hope: Thoughts on Reclaiming the American Dream' was published in 2006, as was 'It Takes a Nation: How Strangers Became Family in the Wake of Hurricane Katrina'. He married Michelle Robinson in 1992; they have two daughters. He is an avid fan of the Chicago White Sox and the Chicago Bears, and plays basketball.

Throughout his life he has battled with the feeling that he does not fit in. He learned that his father had married his mother bigamously, having left a wife and two children in Kenya when he came to Hawaii. When his father returned to Kenya it was with another white woman with whom he had four children. Thus Barack Obama has seven half-brothers and sisters (one of whom is married to a Chinese Canadian) and as he has said "When we get together ... it's like a mini United Nations. I've got relatives who look like Bernie Mac, and ... Margaret Thatcher".

The Rt Hon Dr John Reid PC MP
'A Safe Pair of Fists'

He was born and raised in a small coal mining village in North Lanarkshire, near Glasgow on 8 May 1947, the only child of Thomas, a postman, and Mary, a cleaner in a local factory, both of whom were Roman Catholic.

He was educated at St Patrick's RC High School in Coatbridge but left school at 16, finding various jobs in places such as an oil pipeline and in insurance. In the latter he was assigned to the tenements of the East End of Glasgow and saw poverty of the sort he didn't know existed.

He had never been interested in going to university but this changed when he read 'The Rise and Fall of the Third Reich' by Walter Shirer. Upon finishing the book he took an Open University foundation course and subsequently gained a place at Stirling University, graduating with a BA in History. It was during his time as a student that his interest in politics began. He was elected Rector of the Students Union and for a short time was a member of the Communist Party. He went on to gain a PhD in Economic History.

His verbal power and sharp intellect meant he was quickly noticed and he was offered a job as a researcher in the Scottish Labour Party. He held this position until 1983 when again his quick tongue and strong political views brought him to the attention of Neil Kinnock, the Labour Leader, who immediately offered him a job as his Political Advisor.

In 1986 he became Scottish Organiser of Trade Unionists and a year later was elected MP for Motherwell North, a seat he held for ten years until he took the seat of Hamilton North and Bellshill. In 1989 he became Opposition Spokesman on Children and two years later on Defence. In 1997 he was appointed Minister of Defence, a year later Minister of Transport. He became Secretary of State for Scotland in 1999 and for Northern Ireland in 2001; he was the first Catholic to hold office in Northern Ireland.

In 2002 he was Minister without Portfolio and Labour Party Chair for a year before becoming Leader of the House of Commons and President of the Council. The same year he was made Secretary of State for Health. In 2005 he was elected MP for Airdrie & Shotts and made Secretary of State for Defence. In May 2006 he was appointed Home Secretary and hit the headlines by declaring parts of the organisation "not fit for purpose". He stood down from Cabinet in 2007 following Tony Blair's departure; he was staunchly loyal to him saying, "when Tony Blair asks me to do something, I do it".

He has been Joint Vice-Chairman of the All-Party Group on Azerbaijan, Belize, Russia and Uganda and was a member of the All-Party Groups on the Balkans, Central Asia and Latin America.

He is a life long supporter of Celtic Football Club and in November 2007 became the Club's Chairman. He is an Honorary Professor and Chair of the Institute of Security and Resilience Studies at University College London. He also enjoys reading, crosswords and music; he owns a Gibson acoustic guitar and in 2000 was made an honorary member of 'The Big Elastic Band'. He gave up drinking in the early 1990s after he infamously, in the House of Commons, tried to force his way on to the floor to vote, a security guard, ex-SAS, came forward to stop him and Reid threw a punch; he was wrestled to the ground. He gave up his life long smoking habit in 2002; at one point he was smoking over 100 cigarettes a day. His vice now is chocolate.

He married Catherine 'Cathie' (née McGowan) in 1969, she died suddenly from a heart attack in 1998; they have two sons, Kevin and Mark. He married his second wife, Carine Adler, in 2002.

James Caan
' "Observe the Masses and Do the Opposite" '

Born Nazim Khan in Lahore, Pakistan, in 1960, the year his father came to England to find work. Arriving penniless, and unable to speak English, within two years he could fly his family to London where he had established a business (making leather jackets) and bought a house near Brick Lane. His example of how to do business made a deep impression on Caan who remembers him emphasising the importance of win-win for all and saying "Successful business is not about good transactions, it's about good relationships".

The family expanded to seven children, and they attended a local CofE primary school. In 1971 a fire broke out in the workshop at the top of their home; the family escaped, but lost everything. Fortunately savings for a trip to Pakistan enabled them to buy a house in Forest Gate. Here James attended secondary school, and made money with a paper round and by selling the leather jackets. He was expected to join the family business but his father's expectations were suffocating and he became desperate for independence. So, aged 16, with no qualifications, he left school, moved out of the family home and into a rented flat in Kensington, paid for by Saturday work. Watching 'The Godfather' he realised he could spell his name differently and changed it.

He quickly realised he needed a proper job to survive and he found one as an interviewer at Premier Personnel. Success was swift and he was headhunted by Alfred Marks, and then Reid Trevena. Here he met his wife, and invested £30,000 (obtained via credit cards) in her business. At 24 he was driving a Rolls-Royce Silver Spirit.

In 1985 he founded Alexander Mann a recruitment company with offices in Pall Mall. In reality the respectable Alexander Mann was fictitious and the ritzy address a windowless cupboard. James started cold calling and by putting himself in the place of the person he was ringing created the vacancies he recruited and charged for! In 1993 he co-founded Humana International, an executive headhunting and international franchise. Aged 42, he had sold both companies for millions, and knew he need never work again. Taking a 'gap year' he learnt to fly, to sail and studied at Harvard.

He wanted something to change his life; the answer was his own private equity firm, Hamilton Bradshaw. It can make decisions quickly and typically invests up to £10 million per project; a model he wants to copy in Pakistan, building on the country's entrepreneurial culture. He'll ask any question to drill down and understand a business.

His many accolades include BT Entrepreneur of the Year (2001), PricewaterhouseCoopers Entrepreneur of the Year (2003) and winner of the Entrepreneur category, Asian Jewel Awards (2003). In 2007 he became a member of 'Dragons' Den'.

For him philanthropy is hands on. He saved Barts Hospital's A&E, and 'adopted' a village he visited in Kosovo with Cat Stevens. In Kashmir, after the earthquake, he organised the manufacture of prefab homes for hundreds. The James Caan Foundation helps children; he is a founding trustee of the British Edutrust Foundation, and supports the NSPCC, CARE and Pakistan's Human Development Organisation. He built a primary school in Pakistan, named for his father, Abdul Rashid Khan, and has now started a secondary school. He helps British people of Pakistani descent rediscover their roots by enabling them to work in Pakistan for a year. When he was 'auctioned' for charity the winner bid £5,800 for lunch with him.

He enjoys the rewards of hard work and loves sailing and cars. He and his wife, and their two daughters have homes in Cannes, London and Lahore. In 2007 the family made the hajj, the pilgrimage to Mecca. His future is increasingly linked to philanthropy "Money's great, but ... it's what you do with it that counts".

Gus Christie
'Glyndebourne Opera'

He is the third generation of Christies to be in charge at the Glyndebourne Festival Opera which, this year, 2009, celebrates its 75th Anniversary. The festival was started by his grandfather, John, who was born into a wealthy Devonshire family, was educated at Eton College, and served in the trenches in WWI where he was awarded the MC. After the war John was given the Glyndebourne estate where he began to develop local enterprises.

Augustus, 'Gus' was born on 4 December 1963 and, like his father and grandfather, was educated at Eton. He obtained an Honours degree in Zoology and spent the first ten years of his working life as a freelance wildlife cameraman making films for the BBC and the American market.

Although he had become a director of Glyndebourne at the age of 25, it was not until his father's retirement, in January 2000, on reaching 65, that he took over as Executive Chairman. His elder brother Hector is a full time eco-warrior; he heckled Tony Blair at the 2004 Labour Conference in Brighton in protest at the hunting ban, and was forcibly ejected. Gus is sympathetic to much that Hector fights for, including an absolute commitment to reducing carbon emissions and, in spite of opposition, obtained permission, in July 2008, to build a wind turbine to cover the annual power requirements of Glyndebourne.

He also has another brother, Ptolemy, who has directed opera at The Grange and has introduced opera into prisons, directing all male casts to great acclaim. His sister, Louise, also has opera in her veins, as she sits on the board of Glyndebourne.

His grandfather had built an Organ Room at Glyndebourne so that his organist friend from Eton, Dr Lloyd, had somewhere to play when he was in Sussex. John used the Organ Room to put on amateur opera productions but on one occasion, at the suggestion of a friend, Audrey Mildmay, a professional opera singer was engaged to 'bring a little professionalism to one of these productions'.

John subsequently married Audrey, in 1931; they spent their honeymoon at the opera festivals at Salzburg and Bayreuth. On their return they decided to build a theatre to hold 300 people, and so, on 28th May 1934, the first Glyndebourne Opera Festival began with a two week season consisting of six performances of 'Le nozze di Figaro' and six of 'Così fan tutte'. Although by the time WWII came the Festival was well established, during the war its activities were suspended and the house was turned into a huge dormitory for East London evacuee children and babies. John was made a Companion of Honour, as was his son, Sir George Christie, for their services to opera. Sir George took over as Executive Chairman of Glyndebourne in 1958.

During Sir George's tenure he rebuilt the theatre extending it greatly to accommodate the growing popularity and demand for seats. He raised the necessary funding through sponsorship to create the modern 1,250 seater theatre seen there today.

Each year the Festival runs from the middle of May through to the end of August and is followed by a tour, the first of which took place in 1968. The tour is for about 2 months each year and takes three operas to about seven locations around the country giving the ability for Glyndebourne and opera to be appreciated more widely.

Gus first married Imogen, the grand-daughter of the late poet laureate Sir John Betjeman, in 1993 and they divorced in 2006; they have four sons. Later this year he is to marry the successful opera singer, Danielle de Neise. She, while still a freshman at the Mannes School of Music, became, at the age of eighteen, the youngest artist ever to enter the Metropolitan Opera studio.

Richard Curtis CBE
'Screenwriter, Philanthropist'

He has two older sisters and a younger brother, and was born in New Zealand on 8 November 1956 to Anthony, a Unilever executive, and Glynness. They lived in several countries including the Philippines where, as a child, he recalls seeing vast slums as his driver took him back to a home with a swimming pool. Another early memory, which may have helped inspire his philanthropy, was his mother cancelling the family Christmas in 1968 so that money normally spent on presents and special meals could be sent to the Biafra appeal; Curtis confesses that the real bonus was being able to watch 'Tops of the Pops' which normally clashed with a lengthy Christmas lunch.

In England he won a scholarship to Harrow before going on to Christ Church College, Oxford where he gained a First in English Language and Literature. A former girlfriend at Oxford was Anne Strutt who married Tory MP Bernard Jenkin, hence the many 'Bernards' - the butt of affectionate humour - in Curtis's work. He met Rowan Atkinson at Oxford where they performed together in revue; Curtis realised he was never going to be as good an actor and was far better off writing his own funny lines.

He became a regular contributor to 'Not the Nine O'Clock News', and then worked on 'Spitting Image', 'Blackadder' and 'Mr Bean'. After attending a wedding where a woman officiated, he thought "this is so much more intelligent … in my family it's my mum who cares about who I'm in love with … it was so much more personal and intimate and meaningful that I suddenly got a bee in my bonnet about women vicars". In 1994 he created 'The Vicar of Dibley'.

His film career sky rocketed with the smash hit 'Four Weddings & A Funeral'. His next film, 'Notting Hill', became the biggest grossing British film of all time. He co-wrote the screenplay for 'Bridget Jones's Diary' and made his directing debut with 'Love Actually'. In 2008 he co-wrote an adaptation of the novel 'The No.1 Ladies' Detective Agency' and has written and directed 'The Boat That Rocked', released in 2009.

He has a genius for linking comedy and tragedy to produce something wonderful. Asked about a reference to 9/11 at the start of 'Love Actually' he said "I became very aware that … newspapers painted the world even more dark than ever as though the world is just all full of anger and fury and it seems to me that that isn't so … you report a bullet, you don't report a kiss … I think it's sometimes important to remember as people become more and more depressed about the world around them that love is always there."

He has devoted much of his life to relieving poverty and inequality. After a visit to Ethiopia where he saw aid workers making a difference with practical skills rather than emotional hand wringing, he was inspired to use his skills, brilliant comedy writing, linked to contacts in the media, to co-found Comic Relief, which has raised over half a billion pounds. Realising governments are crucial to making a difference (Bob Geldof told him he raised more money when he had tea with President Mitterand, who subsequently simply adjusted a tax, than with Band Aid and Live Aid combined) he devoted 2005 to the Make Poverty History campaign, including writing the screenplay for 'The Girl in the Café' which won 3 Emmys and for which Curtis was presented with a Humanitas award.

His partner is Emma Freud and they have four children. She edits much of his work, and he dreads finding "CDB" in the margin - "Could Do Better".

Amongst his awards are the Writers Guild of Great Britain Comedy Lifetime Achievement Award, a BAFTA Fellowship and the BAFTA/LA Humanitarian Award. In 1995 he was appointed MBE and in 2000 CBE. He lists his recreations as "too much TV, too many films, too much pop music".

COMIC RELIEF

Felix Dennis
'Poet & Publishing Entrepreneur'

He was born in 1947 in south London. His father left home when Dennis was a child and he grew up in relatively poor circumstances. He attended Harrow College of Art but dropped out and "wasted a great deal of time playing in R&B bands". He started to work in publishing, but in 1971 was convicted in the infamous Oz obscenity trial and went to prison. He was acquitted on appeal and returned to publishing. To raise capital he sold albums which had been sent to him for review at Oz, and by cajoling friends and contacts, managed to set up H Bunch Associates, which became Dennis Publishing. It published comics to start with but within a year was technically bankrupt.

At that point his genius for seizing the moment inspired him to produce 'Kung-Fu Monthly' which capitalised on the movies of Chinese martial arts star, Bruce Lee, who had died the previous year. It took off and was licensed to foreign publishing companies (including a Cantonese edition). There followed magazines dealing with subjects shunned by bigger publishers, such as Sci-Fi and skateboarding. He moved into publications specialising in personal computing and these, together with a subsequent share in computer retailer Micro Warehouse, generated the financial springboard for his publishing empire, which he also established in the US.

Today Dennis Publishing has over 50 titles including 'Auto Express', 'Maxim', 'EVO', 'Inside Poker' and 'The Week'. It is still entirely privately owned (according to his best selling book 'How to Get Rich' you should "Never, never, never, never hand over a single share of anything you have acquired or created …. Nothing. Not one share."). In 2007 and 2008 Dennis Publishing was named by the Sunday Times as one of the UK's Top 100 Best Companies to Work For.

He has always loved magazines but has a gloomy view of their future predicting the demise of the ink on paper industry within the next 50 years due to increasing illiteracy, environmental concerns, a digital media and rising costs.

However, he cheerfully admits that this doesn't worry him in the slightest since "after the life I've led I'm never going to live that long." For 12 years his wealth saw him "totally misbehaving" with a lifestyle of sex, crack cocaine and rock 'n' roll which cost him somewhere around $100million (he thinks but can't be sure).

In the late 1980s he contracted Legionnaire's Disease which, as he remarked, "is especially lethal to coked-up, overweight, cigarette-smoking, malt-whisky-swilling idiots with too much money who believe they are built of titanium." He was lucky to be diagnosed in time and thereafter amended his lifestyle somewhat, although fine wine is a passion.

In 1999 he again survived a life threatening illness. When he recovered he concentrated on writing poetry and his first collection 'A Glass Half Full' was published in 2002. Other volumes of poetry followed and he is now one of Britain's best selling poets. In 2003 he appeared with members of the RSC at Stratford-upon-Avon reading from his work to raise money for the Royal Shakespeare Company. Apart from poetry his other major preoccupation is the 'Forest of Dennis'. He has planted well over 100,000 trees to date and aims to create the largest broadleaf forest in England.

He has a dream lifestyle with homes in Warwickshire, London, New York, Connecticut and Mustique, and plenty of fancy cars and private jets. For him the most important thing this has brought him is time to do what he wants, and in any case "The jets are always rented. If it flies, floats or fornicates, always rent it – it's cheaper in the long run."

Sir Terence Leahy

'Mr Terry Tesco'

Terence Patrick Leahy was born on 28 February 1956 in Liverpool, the third of four sons to Terence Snr and Elizabeth. The family were of Irish Catholic descent, his father was a ship's carpenter during the war but after being invalided out he became a greyhound racer. At the age of 10 he and the family spent a brief time living on a council owned farm where his father was caretaker of the buildings. The family moved to a maisonette in the Lee Park council estate in Belle Vale, Liverpool, when he was 14.

He was educated at Our Lady of the Assumption, a Roman Catholic school, where, inspired by his classroom motto 'The more you know, the higher you go', he won a scholarship to St Edward's College, Everton, a Catholic grammar school. He was the only one of the four children to receive higher education. He studied for a BSc in Management Science at the University of Manchester Institute of Science & Technology, graduating in 1977.

Due to high unemployment in Liverpool he obtained a summer job in Wandsworth, London, aged 17, stacking shelves at Tesco. After graduating from university he took a job as Management Trainee at the Co-Op but shortly afterwards quit and moved with his girlfriend to London.

In 1979 he joined Tesco as a Marketing Executive and by the age of 24 had become a Marketing Manager. By 1986 he was Commercial Director of fresh food and by 1992 Marketing Director, and was appointed to the board of directors. In 1995 he became Deputy Managing Director followed by Chief Executive two years later; he was 41 years old.

His business decisions have seen him turn a once dwindling business into a multi-billion pound profitable, and now worldwide, company. In the early 1990s he brought in Tesco Metro and Tesco Express followed by the company's 'value' brand of goods. In 1995 he launched the Tesco 'Clubcard', this was immediately dismissed by the competition as 'electronic Greenshield stamps'. However it proved successful and Sainsbury's admitted it was wrong and launched its own loyalty card.

Following his appointment as CEO he expanded the company into other sectors such as non-food, banking and financial services, Tesco Extra and began expanding internationally. In the late 1990s Tesco.com was introduced.

During an interview he was asked if he was obsessed? "Yes," he responded "obsessed with the customers, obsessed with the business and obsessed with the people who work in the business. So that is not a bad choice of word". His successful leadership skills have transformed Tesco into one of the biggest retail brands in the UK. Each week he makes surprise visits to the stores to talk to customers, assist and get to know the staff and help stack shelves.

When asked what advice he would give to young people starting out today he said "Choose what you like and make a career out of it. Then you'd have to say 'work hard' because as the old saying goes, it's more about perspiration than inspiration".

His wife, Alison, is a doctor; they have three children, twins, Katie and Tom, and David.

He was knighted in 2002 and also received the honour of the Freedom of the City of Liverpool. In 2003 he was named Britain's Business Leader of the Year and in 2004 was named European Businessman of the Year by Fortune magazine. The same year Management Today named him the most admired leader in the UK. He is a director on the Liverpool Vision Regeneration Board and former Chancellor of Manchester University. He is also an avid football fan, supporting Everton.

Lucy.
TESCO
TESCO
TESCO

Charles Morgan
'Car Builder'

Born into the famous family, creators of the Morgan Car, the last of the truly British designed and built cars. The Morgan Motor Company was formed in 1909 by HFS Morgan, his grandfather; the cars are still built by hand in their factory located in the Malvern Hills.

Charles Peter Henry Morgan was born on 29 July 1951 in Malvern. The only son and youngest of three children to Peter and Jane Morgan (née Christie), he had his father's and grandfather's passion for motor sport, learning to drive in his grandfather's F-type three-wheeler.

He boarded at Oundle School where he says he was more arty than sporty. He remembers that, at the age of 17, he was picked up from school by his father who was driving the Plus 8 prototype which left black tyre marks when he did a standing start wheelie. His friends were very impressed but the masters less so! He went on to Sussex University graduating with a BA Hons in History of Art in 1971 before attending London University where he obtained a Diploma in Film Studies.

Hoping to use his artistic flair to design book covers he went to work in the publishing world, but there he spent his time flogging around London with a heavy bag full of books trying to sell to art colleges and libraries. He soon realised this was not for him and, in 1974, joined ITN as a cameraman where he filmed news such as the departure of the Shah from Iran, the aborted rescue attempt of the US hostages held in Iran, the conflict in Beirut and the Israeli invasion of Southern Lebanon, the transfer of power and the first free elections in Zimbabwe and the collision between an Icelandic gunboat and a Royal Navy frigate during the 'Cod War'.

On another occasion he was with Green Peace filming whaling off Spain with Sue Lloyd-Roberts. They were all arrested, held and interrogated by the police. The policemen questioning Charles knew the Morgan name and cars and when Charles explained that he had a race to attend the next day he was released before the others; but not before Sue managed to slip him the film to take to the studios, which he did, making it to the race just in time.

In 1982 he co-founded Television News Team Ltd where he directed and filmed the Russian conflict in Afghanistan, the first documentary behind Russian lines. He had quite some difficulty extracting himself and eventually managed to follow Eric Newby's route out through the Hindu Kush. Returning to England two stone thinner and not being recognised by his father he felt there must be an easier way of making money!

Hence, in 1985 he became Marketing Manager in the family business. In 1990 he studied a three year part time course at Coventry University where he gained a Diploma in Modern Manufacturing. He also studied for an MBA in Engineering Management, graduating in 1994. In 1999 he became Managing Director and in 2003, following his father's death, became Chairman of the Company.

In 2000 he headed the team that developed the Aero 8, the first completely new Morgan for 30 years, and later the AeroMax. He was appointed Director of 'The LIFE Car Project' with the aim of making the company the first sports car manufacturer with zero emissions.

He won the British Racing and Sports Car Club and British Racing Drivers Club Production Sports Car championships in 1978 and 1979. He drove a factory made Morgan Plus Eight GTR for the 1997 and 1998 FIA International GT series.

He married his third wife, Kira Kopylova, in 2003. He has five children; a son, Xan, by his first wife, two daughters, Harriet and Kate, by his second wife and two more young children Max and Eva, with his third.

Lucy.

Dame Vivienne Westwood DBE RDI
' "I don't like orthodoxy in any shape or form." '

Her childhood was spent in Tintwhistle, close to Lancashire and Yorkshire, with their cotton and woollen industries. She learned early to appreciate the high quality tweeds and knits that would later become the world renowned signature of many of her designs. She was born on 8th April 1941 into an England of war time make-do-and-mend. Her mother could make the family's clothes and her father supplemented his factory wages by making Xmas holly wreaths. Both were keen dancers, something Vivienne also inherited.

From an early age she was not afraid to take a stand against orthodoxy; typically on her first day at school she used the boys' lavatories as there was a queue for the girls'. At Glossop Grammar School she customised her school uniform to include a fashionable pencil skirt.

When she was 16 the family moved to Harrow where her mother ran a post office. Vivienne studied fashion and silversmithing at Harrow Art School, but left because "I didn't know how a working-class girl like me could possibly make a living in the art world." She trained as a teacher, being remembered as "potentially the greatest primary school teacher of her generation." When her class made fish mobiles she first took the children to a fishmonger to see fish.

At a dance she met her first husband, Derek Westwood, with whom she had a son. However, life as a suburban housewife was circumscribed and boring in contrast to that enjoyed by her brother and his friends, amongst whom was Malcolm McLaren who then became her new partner.

Vivienne and Malcolm set up shop at 430 King's Road as 'Let It Rock' selling 1950s memorabilia and clothing. In 1972 it reopened as 'Too Fast to Live Too Young to Die' with leather and motorcycle gear. It also sold T-shirts which Vivienne customised with additional items, including letters made out of chicken bones, attached with chains, spelling out 'Perv' or 'Rock'– these garments are now collectors' items fetching thousands of pounds.

In 1974 the shop became notorious as 'SEX' selling fetish wear and customised T-shirts which were so shocking that Vivienne was once arrested. In 1976 it changed again to 'Seditionaries', the headquarters of punk. At this stage the shop's décor included a live rat. In 1979, it became 'World's End' with an interior resembling a ship complete with sloping decks, and the famous 13 hour clockface showing time going backwards. In 1980 Vivienne's and Malcolm's interests began to diverge. Their partnership came to an end in 1984 when Vivienne moved to Italy with her new business partner Carlo D'Amario.

Vivienne had been making clothes for the shop in all its incarnations, and in 1981 she showed her first collection 'Pirates'. She has been showing innovative collections ever since, undertaking extensive historical research for each of them. 'Harris Tweed' provided the instantly recognisable Westwood logo of the orb (Harris's trademark) surrounded by a Saturn-like ring – symbolising her traditional approach to work combined with a step into the future.

Her clothes shock with their extraordinary contradictions, but supermodels waive their fees if they can keep the clothes they model. Her evening dresses have been worn to the State Opening of Parliament and, as Brintons' ads revealed, she can even make carpets look stunning. They're not cheap but as she said "I think it's really great to buy a wonderful dress and some nice shoes and don't buy a car for example … Buy less and do something great … You have to wear clothes so why not wear beautiful clothes."

She was British Fashion Designer of the Year in 1990, 1991 and 2006. In 1991 she was appointed OBE, and in 2006 DBE for services to fashion. A retrospective of her work has toured the world. In 1992 she married Andreas Kronthaler, 25 years her junior; she has a granddaughter. In 2007 she launched a manifesto 'Active Resistance to Propaganda' to save mankind from mediocrity.

Dr Lavinia Byrne
'Communicator - Writer & Broadcaster'

She was born in Birmingham, into a devout Roman Catholic family, on 10th March 1947. Aged 17, certain of her religious vocation, she entered the Institute of the Blessed Virgin Mary (IBVM) as a postulant. Whilst there she started training as a teacher studying French and Spanish at Queen Mary College, London University. She studied for a Westminster Diploma in Theology, and in 1971 obtained a PGCE from Cambridge. She later gained a post-graduate Certificate in Information Studies. In 1997 she was awarded the honorary degree of Doctor of Divinity by the University of Birmingham.

She taught Modern Languages at several Roman Catholic schools. Whilst teaching at the Bar Convent, York she was asked to look after youngsters whose families had come on retreat. For identification they wore cardboard discs with their names. At the end of the retreat it was suggested that everyone should write on the back of their, now rather tatty, discs the name of a gift they would like. When it came to her turn, Lavinia quite spontaneously wrote "Words"; that moment her vocation changed from teacher to communicator.

In 1980 she undertook a 'Tertianship' (an intense period of training available to those 15 years into religious life) after which she realised secondary school teaching was no longer for her. She started teaching at the Institute of Spirituality, Heythrop College, University of London, and became co-editor of 'The Way' and 'The Way Supplement'. She travelled to North America to meet authors and academics, and started writing books herself.

She began broadcasting with the BBC on 'Thought for the Day', and presenting 'Words of Faith' and the 'Daily Service'. From 1991 - 1995 she was Associate Secretary for the Community of Women and Men in the Church at the Council of Churches for Britain and Ireland, and was later a tutor at Westcott House, Cambridge.

In 1994 she published, 'Woman at the Altar', setting out arguments for the ordination of women as priests in the Roman Catholic Church. It was written before the debate on the subject was closed, and was submitted for approval. However, the Vatican's Congregation for the Doctrine of the Faith wanted it destroyed and in 1998, despite Cardinal Hume's recommendation that no action be taken, copies were burned. In 1999 she went to speak at a conference in Peru. Here she suffered severe altitude sickness and felt close to death. Out of this came the courage to speak candidly about the ordination of women and birth control, and she realised she must leave the IBVM which had to uphold teachings persecuting her and thousands of like minded women.

In 2001 she said "You couldn't get anybody more conventional than me, and yet because of this sense of commitment to God and commitment to the church, I have been led, one step at a time, to a place that is quite radical and which ... puts me in conflict with central authority." On 21st January 2000 the Vatican gave its consent to her petition to leave. It took just 6 weeks for the dispensation to land on her doormat, together with a gas bill and junk mail. She had been a member of the IBVM for 35 years.

She would never consider becoming an Anglican "a birthright Catholic, my parents conceived a Catholic child, they wanted me to be a Catholic, they gave me all the privileges and blessings of being a member of the Catholic church, and I never want to turn my back on that."

Today she writes, leads seminars and is a speaker on lecture tours to various parts of the world, including the Middle East. Away from religion she enjoys cooking and reading detective stories. She suffers from familial tremor for which she underwent successful deep brain stimulation – an X-ray photo of this is included on her website!

The Most Rev & Rt Hon Dr John Sentamu PC
'Archbishop of York – From Uganda with Love'

Britain's first ethnic minority archbishop was born the sixth of thirteen children, on 10 June 1949 into Uganda's Buffalo Clan. Weighing only 4lb it was feared he would not live and he was baptised immediately. But he survived and started achieving early - aged 6 he wrote a prize winning song about the killer mosquito. Educated at Old Kampala secondary school he found studying easy but the 24 mile round trip hard until he was given a bike. He earned the fees he needed to finish school by gardening.

He studied law at Makerere University, Kampala, and at the Law Development Centre. At the age of 24 he was an Advocate of the High Court of Uganda and called to the Bar and the Bench. Under Idi Amin's tyrannical regime he jailed innocent people to save them from summary execution, and was himself arrested after defying an order to deliver a not guilty verdict on a cousin of Amin's. He came to Britain in 1974 after securing a place at Selwyn College, Cambridge to read theology, and trained for ordination at Ridley Hall, Cambridge. A major factor in his decision to become a priest was the murder of his friend, Archbishop Janani Luwum. Nearly 30 years later, in Westminster Abbey, as Archbishop of York, he would launch the Archbishop Janani Luwum Trust.

He served as Assistant Chaplain at Selwyn College, and as Chaplain at Latchmere House Remand Centre. After Curacies in the Diocese of Southwark, he was Vicar of both Holy Trinity, Tulse Hill and St Matthias, Upper Tulse Hill. He became Bishop for Stepney in 1996 and Bishop for Birmingham in 2002. In 2005 he was enthroned as Archbishop of York in a magnificent ceremony in York Minster with African singing and dancing, and with the Archbishop himself playing African drums. He is now Primate of England and Metropolitan, a member of the House of Lords and a Privy Councillor. He is President of both Youth for Christ and the YMCA, and is Chairman of the NHS Haemoglobinopathy Screening Programme. He is also a Fellow of the Royal Society of Arts.

Down to earth and outspoken he was appointed to the Stephen Lawrence inquiry, and chaired the review of the Damilola Taylor murder investigation. Issues close to his heart are young people, the challenge of knife and gun crime, the importance of family, freedom from slavery, injustice and conflict abroad. In 2006 he camped for a week in York Minster in a vigil of fasting and prayer for lasting peace in the Middle East. In 2007, in an interview on BBC1's the Andrew Marr Show, he cut up his dog collar to demonstrate how Robert Mugabe had "taken people's identity and cut it to pieces". He has stated he will not wear it again until Mugabe has gone; the pieces were handed to Andrew Marr for safekeeping.

He married Margaret in 1973; they have two grown up children, and two grown up foster children (whose dying mother asked the Sentamus to care for them). He enjoys music and cooking – his Desert Island Discs luxury was a kitchen – and cooks for staff, including Christmas dinner, and pancakes on Shrove Tuesday. He enjoys sport and visits the gym daily. He replies personally to every letter he receives, and in 2008 helped raise over £100,000 skydiving with the Red Devils for the Afghanistan Trust (www.afghanistantrust.org).

Every day begins with prayer and he quotes Dom Helder Camara, after Martin Luther, "I find these days that I am so busy I have to spend at least four hours each morning in prayer", although he admits he doesn't always manage this.

He also quotes a former Archbishop of Canterbury, Lord Ramsey, who spoke in 1962 of his longing for the day in England when the Church would learn the faith afresh from Christians of Africa and Asia, "I should love to think of a black Archbishop of York holding a mission here, and telling a future generation of the scandal and the glory of the Church."

Lucy.

Rebecca Adlington OBE
'Gold Medallist with a Golden Nature'

Whilst hopeful of a medal in the 800m freestyle, for Rebecca Adlington the Beijing Olympics were intended to be more of a dress rehearsal for the 2012 London Olympics. She wasn't supposed to emerge as Britain's most successful Olympic swimmer in 100 years with 2 Gold medals, or to smash the longest standing world record in swimming, which had been set the year she was born.

However, in two weeks, she went from 'Miss Nobody', a virtually unknown teenager competing in her first Olympics, to leading Team GB off the BA jumbo that brought them home from Beijing.

She was born on 17th February 1989 in Mansfield, Nottinghamshire, the youngest of three sisters. It was, and still is, a close knit family. Her mother, Kay, gave up work to support Rebecca's training with 4.30am alarm calls and two daily round trips to Nottingham. Aged 7 Rebecca started swimming lessons at the local council run Sherwood Baths (due to be renamed in her honour) and was soon racing. By 13 she was training with Bill Furniss, chief coach for Nottingham's Nova Centurion Club. They clicked right away "She always had obvious talent ... and the ability to want to get better ... even from the age of 13 she was determined to be the best she could be." He has also likened her to "a great white shark" in the water.

By 2004 she was a European Junior Champion, but then training stopped. She caught glandular fever with post viral fatigue and also had to deal with her sister's life threatening complications from the same illness. She lost a year but it made her a stronger person and even more determined. By 2008 she was only one second off a world record.

Her Gold medal for the 400m freestyle was unexpected, "Even when I watched it back I thought, it's not Gold, I think something's gone wrong here". The 800m Gold medal was not so unexpected but to smash the world record was. There could even have been three Golds but the Women's Freestyle Relay Team was eliminated in a heat when Rebecca was being rested.

By all accounts she remains totally down to earth, valuing politeness, kindness and fair play, and is unfazed by the publicity which has descended upon her. She doesn't really enjoy all the media attention, and she certainly hasn't got rich - her only commercial sponsor is speedo whose costume she wore in both Gold medal races – sadly she has lost the actual costume.

On her return to Mansfield thousands of well wishers cheered her on in an open top bus tour of the town. The Mayor presented her with a pair of gold Jimmy Choo shoes, fulfilling a promise he had made to her if she won Gold. Well known for her love of shoes Rebecca wore the Jimmy Choos on the BBC's 'Sports Personality of the Year', nearly falling over on the way down a gigantic ramp for an interview as one of the nominees. Typically the stunning red dress she wore was picked up in a little shop in Spain on holiday with her Mum.

She genuinely loves the hard work associated with her sport "I just really love to swim ... it sounds silly but ... I love the satisfaction of doing a hard session and coming out knowing you've given it your all ... I don't get bored with it." Training means 4 hours in the pool every day, except Sunday, plus intensive gym work and daily runs.

She recently called for football players to be subject to the same stringent drug testing regime as any other sporting stars; and when her swimming career is over plans to find a job within the sport to pass something on to the next generation. She was appointed OBE in the 2009 New Year Honours.

Joe Calzaghe CBE
'The Italian Dragon'

The ref holds up the winner's hand – it's a debatable points decision but gold in the European Junior Championships goes to a Romanian, Adrian Opreda. Opposite him, tears running down his face, 17 year old Joe Calzaghe vows never to lose another fight – a promise he keeps.

The man who would one day be described as the greatest British boxer ever, was born on 23rd March 1972 in London to a Welsh mother and Sardinian father. When Joe was two the family moved to Newbridge, South Wales. For Joe the 'dragon' is particularly appropriate being both Wales's national emblem and a mythical beast of Sardinian legend able to kill men with just one look.

His father, Enzo, was keen on sport and at an early age introduced Joe to the local Newbridge Boxing Club. His first punch bag was a rolled up carpet in the family home, and by the time he was nine he was boxing as a southpaw. His father, who had never fought or trained a professional fighter, became his coach. It's highly unusual for a father and son team to progress from amateur to professional status and the experts didn't believe the Calzaghes could make it work. But Joe and Enzo proved them wrong with Enzo keeping his son motivated, getting up, come rain or snow, to run with him – as Joe acknowledged when accepting the 2007 BBC Sports Personality of the Year award "I've got a pain in the bum Dad to thank".

As a boy Joe was small and was bullied at school, "It probably did affect me a little bit and I can sympathise with kids that do get bullied in school, because it's a horrible time to go through … when I was in school I was a totally different person to what I was outside, and obviously when I came to the gym it was my escapism." When he was 14 he told his careers teacher that he was going to be a World Champion – a statement that was met with incredulous laughter.

He won 110 out of his 120 amateur contests with four schoolboy ABA titles and three consecutive Senior British ABA titles - only the second boxer ever to win the welterweight, light middleweight and middleweight titles. He turned professional in 1993 and in 1997 beat Chris Eubank to become WBO Super Middleweight Champion.

He carried on winning but it was not until his 2006 bout with the American Jeff Lacy that he really achieved the recognition he deserved. Despite having injured his hand, and having to be persuaded by Enzo not to withdraw, he won the fight having landed over 1,000 punches. He went on to defeat Sakio Bika and then, in 2007, Peter Manfredo which left the way clear for a bout with the unbeaten Dane, Mikkel Kessler, holder of the WBA and WBC belts. Joe won comfortably on points.

Now it was time for a fight with Bernard Hopkins which was staged in April 2008 in Las Vegas, Joe's American debut. It looked like disaster when Joe hit the floor in the opening round, but he picked himself up and after twelve, gruelling rounds, won on points, becoming WBO Light Heavyweight Champion. Joe followed this up by defeating Roy Jones Jnr in New York's Madison Square Garden.

In February 2009, unbeaten in 46 fights over a 16 year career boxing at two different weights, Joe retired. He is lucky in being unmarked, both physically and mentally, after so many years at the top and now concentrates on boxing promotion and charity work.

He has two sons but confessed on the Jonathan Ross Show that he didn't want them to become professional boxers. In 2003 he was appointed MBE (his mother, who has the same initial, opened the letter thinking it was for her) and in 2008 CBE for services to sport and voluntary services in Wales.

Lawrence Dallaglio OBE
'The Wasp of Wasps'

Eighteen years of rugby, in which he played 85 times for England, came to an end in 2008 when he retired to allow him more time for family and other things he had missed out on during his rugby career. He was a key player in the England team, under Martin Johnson, which won the 2003 World Cup.

He was born on 10 August 1972 at Queen Charlotte's Hospital, London to an Italian father, Vincenzo, and an English mother, Eileen. His older sister, Francesca, died in 1989 in the Marchioness Riverboat disaster on the Thames; he was due to go to that party but had been unwell.

At King's House School in Richmond he was keen on sport, especially football, but he also joined the school choir and learnt the piano. As part of the choir, he sang at the wedding of Andrew Lloyd Webber and Sarah Brightman in 1984. In 1985 the choir went to Abbey Road and sang the backing track on the Tina Turner hit 'We Don't Need Another Hero'.

In 1986 he started at Ampleforth College, North Yorkshire, where, at 16, he started playing Rugby seriously as No 8. He was never a great academic but could have been if he had 'applied himself'. He went to a tutorial college, d'Overbroeck, in Oxford, to complete his 'A' Levels, obtaining two, which enabled him to take up a place at Kingston University where he studied Urban Estate Management.

While at d'Overbroeck he was chosen for the Middlesex rugby team and then the London/South East divisional team, just missing out on the English Schools team. He was later picked for a North of England Schools XV which led to an invitation to join Wasps, initially in the Under-19s Colts team. During the 1992/93 season, when he was nearly 21, he played for the England Under 21s but not in the Wasps first team as competition was fierce.

He was a member of the inaugural World Cup Sevens-winning squad with England in 1993. His debut in the first Wasps team came in the 1993-94 season.

In 1995 Rugby turned professional and many of the Wasps' best players moved to other clubs. This left the door open for Dallaglio and he became Captain. The team went on to win the championship in the first season of professional rugby. In November that year he played his debut game for England against South Africa at Twickenham, winning his first English cap. In 1996 he played his first Five Nations Championship and in 1997 he was chosen to play in the Lions tour to South Africa. The same year he was made England Captain but resigned as Captain in 1999 following a false newspaper story about him.

He was a key player in the winning teams for the 2003 World Cup and the Grand Slam in the Six Nations Championship. He regained the captaincy in 2004 but then announced his retirement. The following year he was called for his third Lions tour to New Zealand but in the opening game was severely injured. He was included in the 2006 Six Nations Championship and also reclaimed the Wasps captaincy; leading the club to its second European Championship win.

He played in the 2007 World Cup where England made, but lost, the final. In 2008 he again announced his retirement from International Rugby ending his career with Wasps winning the 2008 Guinness Premiership Final.

He married his long term partner Alice Corbett in July 2006; they have three children, Ella, Josie and Enzo. He is honorary President for the Middlesex region of the Wooden Spoon, the charity of British and Irish rugby which supports disadvantaged children and young people in the UK and Ireland. In 2008 he cycled 933kms over the French Pyrenees with Warren Smith for the Bliss Charity. He was appointed MBE in 1995 and OBE in 2008.

Dame Tanni Grey-Thompson DBE
'Aim High'

She is one of the world's most successful disabled athletes having won 16 medals at 5 Paralympic Games. She was born, with spina bifida, on 26th July 1969 in Cardiff and although she could walk, using callipers, as she grew her legs were unable to support her body weight, so slowly she became paralysed and had her first wheelchair when she was seven.

One of her personal mottos throughout life has been aiming high. Her autobiography 'Aim High' was published in 2007. Her mother taught her the motto "Aim high, even if you hit a cabbage." It was something her grandfather had taught her mother.

No one ever told her that she shouldn't try and while she was growing up she was never told that there were things she couldn't do just because she was in a wheelchair. Hence, as a Brownie and sitting in her first wheelchair, she tried to skip just like the other Brownies.

She went to St Cyres Comprehensive School and always wanted to play sport, initially basketball but she quickly realised it was not for her. From the moment she started athletics she realised she had found her vocation. It was here that she first tried wheelchair racing and at the age of 15 won the 100 metres at the Junior National Wheelchair Games. Aged 18 she became a member of the Bridgend Athletics Club, the British Wheelchair Racing Squad and was also selected for her first World Wheelchair Games. After graduating from Loughborough University in 1991, with a degree in BA Politics, she joined the Cardiff Athletics Club.

In 1988 she was selected for the national team for the Seoul Paralympic Games. She won her first medal (bronze) in the 400 metres.

Following a year out (after spinal surgery) she competed at the 1992 Barcelona Paralympics, winning four gold medals, a silver and also became the first woman to break the one minute barrier in the 400 metres. The same year she won the first of six London Wheelchair Marathons. Paralympics in Atlanta, 1996, Sydney, 2000 and Athens, 2004 followed during which she accumulated another seven Gold Medals and three Silver. The races ranged from 100 metres to 800 metres.

Her final race, prior to retirement, was at the 2007 VISA Paralympic World Cup in the 200 metres. She has appeared on 'A Question of Sport', 'Weakest Link', 'Mastermind' and has received the Big Red Book on 'This is Your Life'. She has also commentated on sports events on TV and radio and has written articles for journals, magazines and newspapers. She was voted Welsh Sports Personality of the Year three times and has received the Freedom of the City of Cardiff.

In 1999 she married Ian Thompson, and they have a daughter, Carys. Carys is actually Tanni's real name but her elder sister called her 'Tiny', pronounced 'Tanni', which stuck.

She has honorary degrees from 24 universities around the UK, from Newcastle to Southampton. In 1992 she was appointed MBE, the Sunday Times Sportswoman of the Year and Female Disabled Athlete of the Year by the Sports Writers Association. In 2000 she was appointed OBE. She also became BBC Sports Personality of the Year, Welsh Woman of the Year, Welsh Sportswoman of the Year, Best Welsh Sportswoman of 50 years, received a Pride of Britain Special Award and received the Sportswriters Award. In 2001 she was voted UK Sporting Hero by SPORT UK, in 2003 she was inducted into the BWSF Hall of Fame and in 2004 became the BBC Wales Sports Personality of the Year, for the third time. In 2005 she was made DBE, demonstrating that she is a woman of strong determination ruled by integrity, vision, passion, performance and leadership.

Lucy.

Tony O'Shea
'The Silverback'

He was born on 9th May 1961 in Stockport, where he still lives. Despite being internationally famous as a professional darts player, he continues to play in his local darts league. He is currently sponsored by the Mariflex Group of Companies.

In 2002 he competed for the first time in the British Darts Organisation Championships and lost only narrowly to a former Masters champion, Colin Monk. He has reached the final of all four of the British Darts Organisation's Grand Slam of major darts tournaments, but to date he has yet to win one.

In 2007, on his 46th birthday, he achieved a spectacular nine dart finish during the International Darts League. This was also his first televised nine dart finish. A nine dart finish is considered to constitute a perfect game, as a single game (also known as a leg) requires a player to score 501 points, and the minimum number of darts a player has to throw to achieve this is nine. Traditionally a nine dart finish is achieved by throwing 60 (treble 20) with each of the first six darts, leaving 141 to be scored with the remaining three – something missed by many players, but achieved by Tony on this occasion.

In 2003 he won the Swiss Open and was part of the victorious England 4-man team for the World Darts Federation World Cup in France. In 2008 he won the Welsh Masters and was also a semi-finalist in the Winmau World Masters. In 2009 he won the Scottish Open.

Since his agonising defeat in the final of the British Darts Organisation at the Lakeside in 2009 (6 – 7 to 'The Count' Hankey) Tony has been trying to decide whether to stick with the British Darts Organisation, where he can carry on playing international darts, or to switch to the more lucrative Professional Darts Corporation, which is televised by Sky. Earlier he had had a disagreement with the British Darts Organisation about his ranking which started him thinking about a move.

However, he has said that whilst his wallet is telling him to move to the Professional Darts Corporation his heart is telling him to stay with the British Darts Organisation and have another crack at finally winning at the Lakeside.

He still competes on his local circuit at 'The Pineapple Inn' in Marple, Cheshire, and in over nine years has lost just one game. He has won the Cheshire Open four times, the Cheshire Gold Cup Singles three times and the Cheshire Gold Cup Pairs four times. He has also won the Stockport Express Advertiser Open seven times and the Derbyshire Open.

He is right handed and uses a 22g DataDart. His nickname, Silverback, is due to his somewhat squat physique, and his special theme tune when he walks on is DJ Otzi's 'Hey Baby'.

Tony is married to Gill and they have two children, John and Jennifer. To date he has seven grandchildren. He is a golfer (he was formerly a green keeper at Hazel Grove Golf Club) and has achieved a hole-in-one. All his life he has been a fan of Stockport County Football Club, often wearing the club colours, which are blue and white, on stage. He will drape a club scarf round his neck before he is interviewed on television and he often ends these interviews with the fans' call "Blue Army!".

Ronnie O'Sullivan
'Snooker's Mozart'

Whether he is playing right or left handed 'The Rocket' is the world's most exciting and naturally talented snooker player.

His mother, Maria, ran away from home, aged 16, to avoid an arranged marriage, and met Ronnie's father working at Butlins; they married a year later. Ronnie was born in Birmingham on 5th December 1975, and he remembers his parents working non-stop, and being looked after by "loads of different au pairs" until he was 7, when his sister, Danielle, arrived and his mother gave up work. Ronnie is extremely close to his father and would spend hours polishing his car whilst his father worked in the sex shop he had started. The shop prospered and became a chain, and the now affluent family moved to Chigwell, where Ronnie still lives.

He started playing snooker aged 7 and won his first tournament when he was 9. As a child he went to Pontin's festivals where thousands of snooker players competed over the course of a week. His father would hire a chalet for him and a friend, plus the friend's father to keep an eye on them. Ronnie admits his behaviour was less than perfect and by the time he was 10 he had been banned.

He became the youngest amateur ever to make a century break (aged 10), and at 15 he made a max 147 break, again the youngest ever to do so. Although his father never praised him to his face he was already prophesying he would be a World Champion. Amongst those he told was Gazza who recounted the tale to Ronnie years later.

Hating school, he would run out at 3.15, grab his cue, ring for a taxi (he still remembers the number) and be in the club by 3.50. He paid a school friend to do his homework (but not too well!). The only thing that stopped him bunking off was the thought of his father finding out and beating him so hard he would be unable to sit down or, worse still, stopping him playing snooker. He left without taking exams. By the time he was 12 he was playing tournaments nationwide, winning more than his teachers were earning. At 14 he won a Pro-Am at Stevenage, and at 15 had a manager.

At 16 his world was shattered. Competing in the World Amateur Championship in Thailand he got a phone call – his father had been arrested after killing someone in a fight; he was jailed for 18 years. Two years later Ronnie learned his mother had been arrested. She too was jailed, for tax evasion, and, aged 19, Ronnie, who had never had to do a thing for himself, found himself cooking meals and looking after his sister.

A professional at 16, in 1993, he became the youngest ever UK Champion, and the youngest qualifier for the World Championship. His world ranking went from 800 to 57, and his record of 38 consecutive victories still stands. He won the 1994 UK Championship, the 1995 Masters and the 1996 German Open. In 1997 he made the fastest max ever in the World Championship. But, interspersed with the brilliance was a lifestyle of dope, booze and partying. In 1996 snooker's governing body found him guilty of assault and in 1998 he failed a drugs test and lost his Irish Masters title.

In 2000 he entered the Priory, and in 2001, suffering from depression before the World Championship (which he won) he rang the Samaritans. He tried anti-depressants but the thing that really helped was long distance running which he cites as a major factor in changing his lifestyle and returning him to World Champion form in 2004 and 2008.

For the future he has invested in property, and has a shop, 'Viva La Diva' and a management firm, 'Rocket Productions' to help young snooker players. He has three children.

Victoria Pendleton MBE
'Olympic Cyclist'

She won her first major medal in 2005, winning gold in the women's sprint at the World Track Championships. In the 2008 Beijing Olympics she also won gold in the women's sprint. She had been encouraged into cycling from a very early age by her father, Max, who was passionate about it. He was a chef which meant he could train in daylight hours and cook in the evening, earning more from grass track racing than he could as a chef.

She, and her twin brother Alex, were born in Stotfield, Bedfordshire on 24 September 1980; they raced together until they were 16, earning pocket money from their victories. Alex gave up racing and went on to become a graphic designer but Victoria kept on racing. She was spotted by a national coach, Marshall Thomas, who introduced her to the Manchester Velodrome.

Although incredibly keen on cycling she was not yet ready to dedicate her life to it on a full time basis. She decided that following her school days at Fearnhill School, in Letchworth, it would be better to continue with her education and get a proper job. She went to Northumbria University where she studied Sports and Exercise Science obtaining a 2.1 (Hons). However, Marshall Thomas was persistent and brought her in to practice when she had time off.

She was inspired to compete seriously by the gold medal won by Jason Queally on the track at the 2000 Olympics. Following university, and having trained with the British Team, she went straight to the Commonwealth Games, making it to the semi-finals in spite of the fact that "I almost forgot to pedal as the crowd erupted at the start of the time trial".

She then went to train at the UCI World Cycling Centre in Aigle, Switzerland alongside some of her future opponents. She said it was hard to make close friends "because you know that ultimately you want to beat their arses on the track".

In 2003 she finished fourth in the World Championships which she repeated in 2004 but with no improvement in time and she questioned whether she should continue. She was persuaded to try again later that year at the Athens Olympics but she finished ninth and was devastated. She says of the experience "I was totally underprepared to be in a competition at that level, psychologically and physically. I'd been basically thrown to the lions".

However, a year after Athens she won the world sprint title in Los Angeles, which gave her the required boost of confidence necessary to take her on to the following year, 2006, when she won the Commonwealth Games Sprint in Melbourne, and at the British National Track Championships she won Sprint, 500m Time Trial, the Keirin and the Scratch Race.

Similarly in 2007 she won seven major races at the World Track Championships and also the British Track Championships. This stood her in excellent stead ready to compete in the Olympics in Beijing in 2008 where she won Gold for the Sprint. She went on to win five other major races in 2008 and has continued her winning run in 2009, winning the Sprint at the World Track Championships in Pruszkow, in Poland.

In 2008 she caused a stir by posing naked, except for her bike, on the front cover of the 'Observer Sports Monthly' magazine. Although she has little time away from the track she lists sewing, baking cakes and shopping for shoes as some of her favourite pastimes. Like most cyclists she really dislikes inconsiderate drivers and heavy traffic. She was appointed MBE in the 2009 New Year Honours.

Sir Bobby Robson CBE
'Professional Footballer, England Manager'

Born into a mining family on 18th February 1933, by the time he was 15 he was an apprentice at Langley Park colliery. For 18 months he worked underground 7 hours a day, and studied electrical engineering at evening classes. His parents imbued their sons with a work ethic Sir Bobby has never forgotten. So he worked hard at his apprenticeship, but in his spare time and at weekends played football and knew this was where his heart lay.

He played for Langley Park Juniors and was turning out for their U18s, when, aged 17, Fulham offered him a contract. His father insisted he maintain his trade as an electrician, but working full-time, training with professionals three nights a week and playing at weekends was shattering, and his father finally agreed he could give up his trade to concentrate on football.

By 1950 he was in the first eleven. To him Fulham was fun but not a "serious championship-challenging club", and in 1956 he transferred to West Bromwich Albion. In 1962, following unsuccessful salary negotiations, he requested a transfer, was stripped of the captaincy, and rejoined Fulham, who paid £20,000 and doubled his salary.

In 1957, reading a newspaper, he learned he had been picked for England. He was capped for England 20 times, but the 1962 Chile World Cup saw the end of his international career when he chipped an ankle bone (which gave Bobby Moore the chance to join England).

Back in 1959 he had been advised to train as a coach/manager for a career when his playing days were over. After rejoining Fulham he had coached Oxford University's Dark Blues, and in 1967 signed as Head Coach with the Vancouver Royals. Problems with the club saw him return to England to manage Fulham which was heading for relegation. He tried to turn things around, but a year later saw a headline: 'Robson sacked': newspapers had been informed before him that the club no longer required him.

He became manager of Ipswich Town; the start of 13 golden years with a Chairman he adored, the charming, old Etonian, John Cobbold who gave him a free hand, and drank a bottle of champagne if they won and two if they lost. Ipswich won the FA Cup (1978) and the UEFA Cup (1981). Sir Bobby left to manage England, which he did until 1990, taking England to the semi-finals of the 1990 World Cup only to lose in a penalty shoot out.

In 1990 he managed PSV Eindhoven, winning the Dutch League. In 1992 he went to Sporting Lisbon and in 1994 to FC Porto where he won the Portuguese Cup, the Super Cup and the Portuguese League. In 1996 he moved to Barcelona where he won the European Cup Winners Cup, the Spanish Cup and the Spanish Super Cup. In 1998 he managed PSV Eindhoven before returning to England to join his beloved Newcastle United where he stayed until 2004.

He has battled cancer since 1992. In 1995 an operation to remove a melanoma left him with a hole in the roof of his mouth; in 2006 he was treated for lung cancer, and had a brain tumour removed causing partial paralysis; lung cancer returned in 2007. The Bobby Robson Foundation focuses on early detection and treatment of cancer, and clinical trials.

He married Elsie in 1955, and they have three sons. He has honorary degrees from the Universities of East Anglia and Newcastle, and is in the English Football Hall of Fame (2003). He was granted the Freedom of the City of Newcastle (2005) and received a BBC Sports Personality of the Year Lifetime Achievement Award (2007). In 1990 he was appointed CBE and in 2002 was knighted. A statue of him stands outside Ipswich Town's ground, and in 2008 he was granted the city's Freedom.

Bill Bryson OBE
'Author & "England's Favourite Adopted Son"'

He was born in Des Moines, USA "because somebody had to be" on 8 December 1951, "third child, second son, first superhero" according to his memoir 'The Life and Times of the Thunderbolt Kid' in which he affectionately chronicles growing up in old fashioned, small town America as it made the transition to the space age.

Taking time out from university he backpacked around Europe, arriving in the UK in 1973. Working at a psychiatric hospital in Surrey he met a nurse, Cynthia, and "kind of fell for her, fell for Britain simultaneously". They married and settled in the UK. In 1995 the family moved to New Hampshire, USA; in 2003 they returned to the UK and now live in Norfolk.

Journalism was in his blood, both parents and a brother were journalists, and he always knew he would work with words. He started in Fleet Street, but really wanted to write books. One summer, after he had complained about commuting, his wife rang him at work to say she had put their house up for sale. An offer of the asking price saw him move to Yorkshire, with his wife and four children, to begin life as a full-time writer. He has said "I hoped I would survive … I needed to make … £12,000 year, and I figured if I could do that … we could just about hang on, and for the first couple of years that's about what I did …. Then I got really successful and in a way it was disappointing because life became a lot simpler, I really kind of liked being poor."

Starting with 'The Lost Continent' his travel books became bestsellers, including 'Neither Here Nor There', 'Notes From a Small Island', 'A Walk in the Woods', 'Notes from a Big Country' and 'Down Under'. In 2003 a poll asked which book best encapsulated what it means to be British, the winner was 'Notes from a Small Island'.

One night, flying over a moonlit Pacific, he was struck by how little he knew about our planet and how we evolved from the Big Bang, all of which "had got to be a good story" but which he could only recall seeing portrayed in desperately dull textbooks. He decided to devote part of his life (three years of extensive reading and interviews with scientists), to finding out if it was possible to understand and enjoy science at a level neither too esoteric nor too superficial.

The result – the phenomenally successful 'A Short History of Nearly Everything'. Here nothing is dull: for example, static on TV screens contains ancient cosmic radiation from the Big Bang so don't complain that there's nothing on as you can always watch the birth of the universe. In 2004 it won the £10,000 Aventis Prize for best general science book (which Bryson donated to Great Ormond Street). It also won the EU Descartes Prize for Science Communication; accepting the award Bryson said "Never has someone been more generously awarded for his ignorance".

His writing makes you laugh out loud with its benign self deprecation, which is never malicious, but which pinpoints idiosyncrasies and absurdities with ruthless accuracy. Work for charity includes 'Bill Bryson's African Diary', royalties from which go to CARE International. He has participated in the Tresco Marathon in aid of Cystic Fibrosis, and launched a campaign on behalf of St Martin-in-the-Fields. He is a supporter of Help the Aged.

In 2004 he was appointed a Commissioner for English Heritage. In 2005 he became Chancellor of Durham University, and in 2006 was appointed an Honorary OBE. He is now President of the CPRE where he launched "Stop the Drop" saying "Litter is a problem that doesn't just anger me, it saddens me, especially in Britain because this is such a beautiful country." Or as he put it in an address to graduates of the University of Leicester "When you're walking down the street and you see someone drop litter, kill them."

A Walk
in the
Woods
BILL BRYSON
LUCY.

The Rt Hon The Baroness James OBE
'The Art of Murder'

Author of perfectly crafted crime novels PD James started writing in her thirties when she realised that unless she got on with it she would end up telling her grandchildren she had really wanted to be a novelist. Her first book, 'Cover Her Face', was planned on commuter journeys and written in the early morning before work, at weekends, and in between visiting her husband in hospital and evening classes.

A lucky train of circumstances led to an agent, Elaine Greene, and Faber & Faber who were looking for a new crime writer. The reviewers were enthusiastic, although most assumed the author was male. She had not intended this but recalls that having written down Phyllis James, Phyllis D James and PD James decided the latter "was enigmatic and would look best on the book spine".

She was born on 3rd August 1920 in Oxford. She loved her parents but her childhood was not always easy. A happy early memory is of her mother reading her comics. One morning she simply found the shapes under the pictures made sense; she could read.

Her schooldays are remembered affectionately, the British School, Ludlow where the headmaster loved poetry (she made her detective, Adam Dalgliesh, a poet) and Cambridge County High School for Girls. Dalgliesh takes his surname from PD James's English teacher, Miss Dalgliesh. Years later she learned from her teacher that her father's Christian name had also been Adam.

At 16 she entered the Civil Service, choosing to work in the tax office, which was disastrous. She then joined the Festival Theatre, Cambridge where she met her husband, Connor, who was training to be a doctor. They married in 1941, five days after she came of age. He came home after WWII mentally ill and was never really well again so PD James became the breadwinner. Connor died in 1964 and she has said she "never found, or indeed looked for, anyone else with whom I have wanted to spend the rest of my life."

She worked in the NHS and gained a diploma in hospital administration. After her husband died she entered the Home Office. Here she was extremely happy working in the police and criminal justice departments, and gaining an invaluable understanding of how the forensic service was organised as well as many later opportunities for expert advice.

She takes three years to produce each book, eighteen months plotting and planning and eighteen months writing; worrying for her readers as she nears 90. She is strongly affected by her surroundings so the setting comes first, creating the atmosphere which in turn influences the characters and the plot. Visiting St Barnabas Church, Oxford she had a vivid mental picture of two dead bodies – all of which was relocated to London for 'A Taste for Death'.

Her non detective books include 'The Children of Men' (a terrifying picture of a future where the human race seems to be infertile) and 'Time to be in Earnest', an autobiographical record of 1997/98, a wonderful narrative of a life filled to the brim with family, friends, work, travel, an extraordinary number of outside interests and talks and lectures.

Her many public appointments have included being a Governor of the BBC. She has been awarded numerous literary prizes and seven honorary degrees, and is an Honorary Fellow of St Hilda's College, Oxford, Downing College, Cambridge, Girton College, Cambridge and Kellogg College, Oxford. In 1983 she was appointed OBE and in 1991 was created Baroness James of Holland Park. Her portrait is in the National Portrait Gallery. She has two daughters, five grandchildren and seven great-grandchildren. Her favourite author is Jane Austen.

PD
JAMES

Joanna Trollope OBE
' "Nobody of any age can resist What Happens Next" '

She arrived in her grandfather's Cotswold Rectory on 9th December 1943, the eldest of three children. Her father ran a "small, eccentric but extremely successful building society" whilst her mother was an artist and author.

Educated at Reigate County School for Girls she was "swotty but extremely average", and her headmistress told her parents "I hope you're not expecting university for Joanna, and certainly not Oxford or Cambridge because it's really not at all possible". She won a scholarship to St Hugh's College, Oxford to read English.

She worked at the Foreign Office, and then trained as a teacher. Married with two daughters she began writing part-time when the children were in bed, becoming a full-time writer in 1980. Her first books were a series of historical romances under the pseudonym, Caroline Harvey (an amalgam of family names). To date she has written 14 contemporary novels (four of which have been adapted for television) as well as 'Britannia's Daughters', a study of women in the British Empire. Her books are available in nearly 30 languages and sell in millions.

Her first novel was written when she was 14, in three fat spiral bound notebooks. It is now kept firmly under lock and key, as she says she could not bear her children to find it until after her death when they can "fall about with all the mirth they like". Although not a direct descendant of Anthony Trollope she is distantly related, and at first she resisted reading him. She now admires him hugely and agrees with his view that nobody gets closer to a reader than a novelist.

For her the inspiration for a new novel is the bit of grit in the oyster shell that gets built on; she is extremely alert to the public's current preoccupations at any given moment to provide that first bit of grit. Despite the fact that Agas are rarely mentioned in her books she is resigned to the Aga Saga tag. Her novels are certainly not warm and cosy, dealing as they do with all human emotions and difficult topics, from adoption and lesbians to mistresses and broken families. Relationships are what fascinate her, both within traditional families as well as within the new, extended family settings of the late 20th and early 21st centuries. As she has said you learn more about your fellow humans from fiction than from non-fiction, citing Tolstoy's 'War & Peace' as a better way of finding out about Napoleon's retreat from Moscow than the 'Cambridge History of the Napoleonic Wars'.

As a writer her meticulous research has included working in a supermarket, for 'The Rector's Wife', and staying in Charleston, immersing herself in the atmosphere of America's Deep South for 'Girl from the South'. Much to her surprise a passion for football came out of her novel 'Friday Nights', and she now finds herself "completely addicted". For the same book despite being "decades too old" she also went clubbing which was "memorable".

She does a lot for charity, in a very practical way saying "I've found a powerful speech aimed at a roomful of men, seems most effective in getting them to reach into their pockets, rather than being photographed with 'dear disadvantaged children'." She is a Patron of the March Foundation and Mulberry Bush which work with disadvantaged children, and also of for Dementia (her father was a sufferer). She supports the RNIB and the Right to Read Campaign, the Meningitis Trust, Macmillan Nurses, Breast Cancer Care and the Gloucestershire Community Foundation. In 2007 she joined Channel 4's 'Lost for Words' campaign encouraging children to read. She has chaired the Costa Book Awards and is a judge for the Melissa Nathan Award. In 1996 she was appointed OBE for services to literature. Married twice she now lives alone in London, and is a grandmother.

Rory Bremner
'The One Man Opposition'

Not only can he produce over 100 pinpoint accurate impressions of the famous, he can even impersonate one in the style of another, witness Home Secretary, Jacqui Smith, as Pam Ayres putting a poetic case for extending detention without charge from 28 days to 42 days.

Rory was born on 6th April 1961 in Edinburgh, the younger of two brothers. His father, Major Donald Bremner, was already in his 50s by the time Rory arrived and died when he was 18. Rory was educated at Wellington College, and went on to study French and German at King's College, London. He started his career as an impressionist with impersonations of teachers, sports commentators and Scottish singer, Moira Anderson. A natural show off he progressed from entertaining school friends to stand up work on the comedy circuit, and in 1986 had a sell out run at the Edinburgh Festival.

He was offered a series by the BBC, 'Now Something Else' which ran for seven years. In 1992 he switched to Channel 4 with the award winning 'Rory Bremner – Who Else?' followed by 'Bremner, Bird and Fortune'. Other programs include specials such as 'Blair Did It All Go Wrong?', 'My Government and I' and 'Between Iraq and a Hard Place'. In 2008 Bremner, Bird and Fortune created the brilliant satirical documentary series on the financial crisis, 'Silly Money'.

He doesn't just use his voice for his impressions, physical characteristics are also ruthlessly skewered and incorporated. This caused some offence when he imitated the way in which the eyes of blind politician David Blunkett roll as he speaks. However, when Blunkett wrote "I am deeply relaxed about the impression that Rory does of me," Rory, as a good satirist, was also offended. In 2001 he received the ultimate accolade for a satirist – he was banned from Labour's election campaign bus. In 2005 Bremner picked up the phone and, impersonating Gordon Brown, fooled the then Foreign Secretary, Margaret Beckett, into making highly indiscreet comments about Labour colleagues.

An episode of BBC1's 'Who Do You Think You Are?' showed Rory learning about a father he had never known well. In a moving scene he met a man who had known his father in his prime, fighting in Holland in WWII, who said "You can be very, very proud of your father… you can consider your father as an army on his own." The parallels between his own life, and those of his father and grandfather and their absences when their children were young made a deep impression "I'm late 40s, I've got daughters of 7 and 5 and maybe I'm away too much… I worry about history repeating itself… oh well I'll be around when they're older, but it's not always when they're older that counts, so it's a reminder of the importance of family."

A strong defender of the freedom of speech he wrote in The Independent of the Orwellian destruction of civil liberties in the UK brought about by 25 new Acts of Parliament, citing examples such as a man arrested for an illegal demonstration, when he held up a placard opposite Downing Street bearing Orwell's words "in a time of universal deceit, telling the truth is a revolutionary act"; or the woman prosecuted for causing "alarm, harassment and distress" to US servicemen by displaying a sign saying "George W Bush? Oh dear".

Much in demand as an after-dinner speaker he lists his recreations as cricket, golf, opera and travel. He is married to Tessa, a sculptor, and they have two daughters. He and Tessa met working for the charity 'Tusk Trust' of which he is a Patron. He proposed to Tessa in the romantic setting of a mountain restaurant in Portugal, only just making it there as, with his mind on other things, he had filled his beloved 1963 red Alfa Giulia Spider with diesel instead of petrol.

Johnny Depp
'High School Dropout to Captain Jack Sparrow'

This extraordinary actor, famed for highly individual, sometimes morbid, roles was born in Kentucky on June 9th 1963 into a working class family descended from Cherokee, Irish and German ancestors.

His childhood was troubled. The family kept moving - by the time he was 15 they had lived in 20 different places – and when they finally settled in Florida his parents divorced. Depp stayed with his mother to whom he remains close. When he was 12 he was given a second hand guitar which he taught himself to play, having first stolen a chord book. He started playing in bands in nightclubs where they had to sneak him in as he was under age.

He was a wild child – not fitting in, taking drugs (by the age of 14 he says he had tried everything) and accidentally setting fire to himself. He dropped out of school when he was 15. Two weeks later he returned, but the Dean told him they didn't want him back, and since music was the only thing he had ever applied himself to he should concentrate on that.

At 20 he married and moved to California with a band, The Kids, looking for a record deal. It didn't work and at one point Depp was reduced to telemarketing, selling pens. Then he met actor Nicholas Cage, who introduced him to his agent. This led to a role in 'Nightmare on Elm Street' (the director's daughter saw Depp's audition and told her father to use him).

At this point acting was simply a means of making money so he could continue as a musician. Then the band broke up, so he decided to keep on acting and enrolled at acting school. His first break was '21 Jump Street', which he only did for the money thinking it would be a one shot TV series. However, it took off and he became a teen idol. For three years he played cop Tom Hanson and hated it, feeling totally owned by a corporation, churning out assembly line programmes with no control over his life.

He decided he would only undertake roles he really wanted to do and if he failed he'd go back to pumping gas and playing the guitar. Accordingly he played bad boy Wade "Cry Baby" Walker in 'Cry Baby' and then the bizarre title role in 'Edward Scissorhands', which earned him a Golden Globe nomination. This was his first collaboration with Tim Burton who has become his closest friend, and has directed him in several films, including 'Sweeney Todd'.

His role as Captain Jack Sparrow in the 'Pirates of the Caribbean' films cemented his status as a major film star. Of the characterisation he used for the brilliantly outrageous Sparrow he has said "I was thinking about pirates in the seventeenth century, and … what would the equivalent be in today's world … I thought it would be a rock and roll star, and for me the greatest rock and roll star of all time is Keith Richards." The director has said he thinks the characterisation has links to Depp's own personality.

He was divorced in 1985 and thereafter had several highly publicised relationships, including ones with Winona Ryder and Kate Moss. These were wild times with narcotics and brushes with the law. Then in 1998 he went to France and across a room saw a "wonderful back" – it belonged to French singer and actress Vanessa Paradis. With her he found stability and they have been together ever since. They have two children, and homes in the States, France (complete with vineyard) and in the Bahamas, where Depp bought an island.

In 2007 his daughter nearly died. When she recovered he donated £1 million to Great Ormond Street Hospital where she had been treated. Later, unknown to the public, he had his Captain Jack Sparrow costume flown over and spent time at GOSH with sick children telling them stories, dressed in character.

Clint Eastwood
'Old West Action'

In 1964, reading Variety, Clint noticed that a new Italian release 'Per Un Pugno di Dollari' was doing sensational business. Under the impression the film he'd just made in Europe was called 'Il Magnifico Straniero' he didn't make the connection until he saw a poster for "'A Fistful of Dollars' starring Clint Eastwood" - the first of the "Dollar Westerns" that changed his life.

Although best known as an actor he is just as much a director and producer. His five Oscars include two Best Director for 'Unforgiven' and 'Million Dollar Baby'. His films always come in on time and within budget, and typically include handheld camerawork and outdoor locations rather than studio sets. He formed his own production company, Malpaso, to give him more control over his career and to make the films he wanted.

He was born (weighing over 11lbs) in San Francisco on May 31st 1930. It was the Depression, times were hard and the family moved around, but the one piece of furniture they always took along was great grannie's piano. Aged 9 Clint could play by ear - when he found all the girls gathered round him as he played at a party he started practicing and by 15 was playing at a saloon for food and beer.

He was only once cast in a school play and was so scared when it came to curtain up he swore he'd never do anything like it again. After graduation the family moved to Seattle and he worked stoking furnaces. He planned to study music but was drafted and posted to Fort Ord, California, as a swimming instructor. Fellow servicemen encouraged him to try acting again, so when he enrolled at LA City College he took acting classes in the evening.

The classes got "under his skin" and in 1954 he signed with Universal playing parts in B movies. Then someone decided his Adam's Apple was too big and fired him. Clint kept on acting, supporting himself digging swimming pools between parts.

Then luck stepped in - visiting a friend at CBS he was spotted by an executive who decided he was the ultimate cowboy and cast him in 'Rawhide'. Some years later he was contacted by an Italian agency for a western to be made in Spain – the start of the spaghetti westerns for which Eastwood provided the character's distinctive poncho, hat and cigars.

The world's longest running movie star his many roles include 'Dirty Harry', the offbeat 'Every Which Way But Loose' and a portrayal of John Huston in 'White Hunter, Black Heart'. Directorial work includes 'Play Misty for Me', 'Bird' and 'Million Dollar Baby' as well as 'Flags of Our Fathers' and 'Letters from Iwo Jima'. In 2008 'Gran Torino' made Eastwood the oldest actor ever to reach box office No 1.

He lives in Carmel, where he has been Mayor, and is part owner of Pebble Beach Golf Country Club. He has been quoted as saying "They say marriages are made in Heaven. But so is thunder and lightning" - married twice, divorced once, he's been married to Dina since 1996, and has seven children by five women, as well as two grandchildren older than his youngest child.

Apart from Oscars his awards include five Golden Globes and a Screen Actors Guild Award. In 2007 he became a Chevalier de la Légion d'Honneur. Nearly 80, he's still ready to try something new - "Life is a constant class and once you think you know it all you're due to decay … I have to keep challenging myself and try something I haven't done before." This included learning to climb mountains in the 'The Eiger Sanction'.

He writes and performs his own film music, and has an Honorary Doctorate of Music from Berklee College of Music. What if he'd pursued music? "I might be making a dollar and a half tip in some late night joint instead of making movies … because a person has to know their own limitations."

Sir Michael Gambon CBE

'The Great Gambon'

One of the greatest actors of our time, he was born on 19 October 1940 in Dublin, the eldest of three children to Edward and Mary. At the age of 5 the family moved to Mornington Crescent, London where his father, an engineer, obtained work rebuilding London after World War II. In 1955 they moved to Crayford, Kent.

His parents were devout Catholics so he was educated at St Aloysius Boys' School, serving as an altar boy, before going to St Aloysius' College in Highgate and then to a school in Kent, leaving at 15 with no qualifications. He obtained an apprenticeship as a toolmaker becoming a qualified engineer by the time he was 21.

One day, during his apprenticeship, he noticed a sign 'Backstage Help Required' hanging outside the Erith Playhouse; here he helped in the evenings while still working during the day in the factory. Whilst at Erith he realised that acting was his vocation and hence, at the age of 19, he joined the amateur Unity Theatre in Kings Cross. Following his first paid acting job at the Royal Court he wrote several letters, including one to Hilton Edward saying, "I am flying to New York and passing through Dublin, could I come and see you?". So he went to see him and when asked what he had played, he said "Marchbanks in the West End". Edward clearly knew this to be untrue and said "Well, I can't offer you any good parts but would you play the Second Gentleman of Cyprus (in 'Othello')? Gambon said he would love to and in 1962, his acting career started at the Gaiety Theatre in Dublin.

Later back in England he wanted to join the Old Vic and to do so had to audition for Laurence Olivier. Being so green about the theatre he had not realised that Olivier had acted Richard III to great acclaim and when at the audition, Olivier asked him what he was going to act, Gambon responded "Richard III", Olivier responded, "which part?", "The King" Gambon replies. "What a cheek" says Olivier but after a short audition in which

Gambon manages to tear his hand on a nail, and is patched up by Olivier, he is offered a job. Four years later and on a recommendation from Olivier he joined the Birmingham Repertory Company where he immediately gained title roles in the productions of 'Othello', 'Macbeth' and 'Coriolanus'.

It was 1968 when he was finally spotted by television producers and offered a role in the popular series 'The Borderers'. Television and theatre performances continued including 'The Life of Galileo' (1980) as Brecht, to great success, even the other actors gave him a thunderous ovation. In 1982, he performed in two plays simultaneously, while playing a matinee performance in 'King Lear' he also played in the evening performance of 'Antony & Cleopatra', opposite Helen Mirren. It was his performance in the television series 'The Singing Detective' (1986) that brought him fame and his first BAFTA. He won his second BAFTA as Squire Hamley in 'Wives and Daughters' in 1999, his third as John Harrison in 'Longitude' in 2000 and the following year his fourth as Raymond in 'Perfect Strangers'.

He will of course be remembered by most of us playing Dumbledore in the third and subsequent Harry Potter films, taking over from Richard Harris.

He married Anne Miller in 1962; they have a son, Fergus. In 2007 he became a father for the second time with his long term girlfriend Philippa Hart. He was appointed CBE in 1990 and knighted in 1998.

He is a qualified amateur pilot and has a love of cars. While appearing on the BBC's 'Top Gear' he drove the car so aggressively that it launched into the air on the last corner; the corner was subsequently named "Gambon" in his honour.

Jerry Faye Hall
'Texan Supermodel'

Probably the best known American model, turned actress, she says she adores acting, "Now I have discovered what it's about, I want to do it more and more. I'm hooked on it. It's better than sex. You can do it eight times a week and still you don't get pregnant."

She was born in Gonzales, Texas on 2 July 1956 but shortly thereafter moved to Mesquite, a suburb of Dallas. Her father was a long-haul truck driver and served under General Patton in WWII. She had a poor and turbulent upbringing, which is perhaps why she says "if you come from a poor background and your husband is rich and famous, and you have a fabulous life, it's hard to give it up."

She attended North Mesquite High School where she was an excellent student in most subjects, graduating with honours. English, however, eluded her and it was not until years later that she found out she was dyslexic. In spite of the family poverty she did have a pet alligator, Nathan, which bit her leaving a small scar.

At the age of 16, she moved to France to pursue a modelling career. On the first day she arrived, after buying a new pink metallic crocheted bikini and hitting the beach, she was approached by a fashion agent. She never looked back and soon after moved to Paris where, for a while, she shared an apartment with the singer Grace Jones. It was here that she met fashion illustrator Antonio Lopez where her modelling career really began. She appeared on many magazine covers including 'Vogue' and 'Cosmopolitan'. It was while being paid to appear on the cover of Roxy Music's album, 'Siren', in 1975 that she met Bryan Ferry. She later appeared in their 'Let's Stick Together' video. She has also been the face of Revlon and Yves Saint Laurent Opium perfume.

Motherhood was of greater importance to her than acting but she has appeared in a number of films since the 1980s including 'Urban Cowboy' (1980), 'Topo Galileo' (1987), 'Batman' (1987) alongside Jack Nicholson, 'Vampire in Brooklyn' (1995) and 'Tooth' (2004). Her theatre performances include the Broadway and West End production of 'The Graduate' in 2001, where she played Mrs Robinson to much acclaim, 'Picasso's Women' (2002) in Brighton and again on the West End stage in 'High Society' (2005). She currently holds the world record for the most theatre appearances in one night: 'Les Misérables', 'Phantom of the Opera', 'Chitty Chitty Bang Bang', 'Blood Brothers' and 'Anything Goes'.

A lover of science she buys the New York Times science supplement and the 'New Scientist' and 'Scientific American'. She has an IQ of 146 and has completed an Open University course in Humanities. She has always had a love of poetry and now writes her own, her first published one appeared in The Independent in 2007. Her other love is horses and she often rides near her home in Richmond Park.

She was engaged to Roxy Music's front man, Bryan Ferry, but in 1979 left him for legendary rocker, Mick Jagger. She married him in a Hindu ceremony in Bali in 1990; they have four children, Elizabeth, James, Georgia and Gabriel. The marriage was annulled in 1999 on the grounds that it was not legal under English law.

In addition to her home on Richmond Hill she has a ranch in Lone Oak, Texas and a house in the South of France. In 1985 she published her first autobiography, 'Jerry Hall's Tall Tales'. Her second autobiography is due to be published very shortly.

Recounting advice received from her mother she says; "My mother said it was simple to keep a man, you must be a maid in the living room, a cook in the kitchen and a whore in the bedroom. I said I'd hire the other two and take care of the bedroom bit."

Penelope Keith CBE DL
'More than just a Good Life'

One of the UK's best loved actresses. Despite being known for a posh accent she had a humble, quite difficult start in life, although typically she never agonises about this believing "You succeed in spite of your life, not because of it. I'm a glass half full person".

She was an only child, born on 2 April 1940 in south London. When she was very little her father left and her mother remarried. Aged 6 she went to a convent boarding school in Seaford, Sussex which was keen on drama, often winning the Brighton Festival. She had apparently already decided to be an actress by the time she was five, mainly because nuns (her other career choice at the time) couldn't wear pretty clothes. Early elocution lessons gave her good diction, something she is still passionate about, and she attended the Webber Douglas Academy of Dramatic Art, London, having previously been rejected by another drama school for being too tall.

Her first professional appearance was at the Civic Theatre, Chesterfield in 1959 and thereafter she played roles in repertory until, in 1963, she joined the Royal Shakespeare Company. Nearly five decades of stage performances have taken her across the country in many plays, including 'The Norman Conquests', 'The Millionairess', 'Hobson's Choice', 'The Deep Blue Sea', 'The Merry Wives of Windsor', 'The Importance of Being Earnest', 'Mrs Warren's Profession', 'Time and the Conways' and 'Blithe Spirit'. In 2007 she appeared again in 'The Importance of Being Earnest' to critical acclaim. She has also turned her hand to directing with 'Relatively Speaking' (1992) and 'How the Other Half Loves' (1994).

Although she had previously appeared on television it was not until she played Margo Leadbetter (originally a supporting role) in 'The Good Life' that she became a household name. She then appeared in 'The Norman Conquests' before playing Audrey fforbes-Hamilton in the highly successful 'To the Manor Born' (nearly 24 million watched the final episode). Several other TV series followed, and she has appeared as a guest on 'Wogan' and 'The Morecambe & Wise Show'. Radio work has included the 'Agatha Raisin' series based on MC Beaton's novels.

She is passionate about gardening, having far more in common with Barbara from 'The Good Life', with her own chickens and, long before it became fashionable, a passion for recycling. In 1984 a rose was named after her. She married Rodney Timson, formerly a policeman, in 1978 and they have two adopted sons. She is exceedingly private and refuses to discuss her personal life believing that actors should be "a blank page that the writer writes on".

She believes in giving back to the community and does so in a very practical way with a formidable list of appointments to both national and local foundations and charities. For six years she was a member of the Human Fertilisation and Embryology Authority and in 2002/2003 was High Sherriff of Surrey. In 1989 she became Governor of Queen Elizabeth's Foundation for the Disabled and in 1990 President of The Actors' Benevolent Fund; she is also a Trustee of The Theatres Trust. She is Patron of many organisations, including the Yvonne Arnaud Theatre, the Surrey Hills Area of Outstanding Natural Beauty, the Milford and Villages Day Centre and the Crime Diversion Scheme at HM Coldingley Prison. She is a Deputy Lieutenant of Surrey, and was involved in raising money for an air ambulance for Surrey, and in launching the UK Forces Gulf Fund.

She has won two BAFTAs and has twice been named Variety Club of Great Britain, Show Business Personality of the Year. In 1989 she was appointed OBE, and in 2007 CBE in recognition of her work with charities. Today, home really is a manor house – a 17th century one in Surrey.

Hugh Laurie OBE
'Actor, Comedian, Writer - Dr Gregory House MD'

James Hugh Calum Laurie was born on 11 June 1959 in Oxford. The youngest of four children to Patricia and William George Ranald Mundell 'Ran' Laurie. His father, a doctor, won an Olympic Gold Medal in the 1948 Games for rowing (this was kept in a sock in the bottom of a cupboard, and for a long time Hugh didn't even know of its existence).

Laurie's parents were from a Scottish Presbyterian tradition and he has recalled his mother as "Presbyterian by mood" in that she was suspicious of pleasure, a feeling he says he may have inherited. He speaks very admiringly of his father, but portrays a more difficult relationship with his mother. In an interview he recalled winning a prize, aged 9, and seeing his parents, as his name was read out, look at each other and smile, the first time he felt he had done something that really pleased them.

He was educated at the Dragon School, Oxford, and then attended Eton where he excelled at rowing. He planned to study medicine, but actually followed his father to Selwyn College, Cambridge to read anthropology and archaeology. He admits that rather than study he concentrated on rowing, achieving a Blue in the 1980 Oxford v Cambridge Boat Race. After contracting glandular fever he stopped rowing and joined the Footlights (President, 1981). Here he met Emma Thompson who introduced him to Stephen Fry, and together they produced 'Cellar Tapes' which won the Perrier Award at the 1981 Edinburgh Festival.

He started co-writing and performing sketches for television with Ben Elton and Stephen Fry in 'Alfresco' and 'A Bit of Fry & Laurie'. He was one of the stars of the 'Blackadder' series, and portrayed Bertie Wooster to Stephen Fry's Jeeves in the series based on PG Wodehouse's novels. His screen career has produced roles in films as varied as 'Peter's Friends', 'Sense and Sensibility', '101 Dalmatians', the 'Stuart Little' films and 'Street Kings'. He has also done voiceovers in children's films, including 'Valiant' and 'Monsters v Aliens'.

However, Laurie's most famous role to date is the brilliant maverick Dr Gregory House in the US television series, 'House', which has brought him worldwide fame, including a nomination as the second sexiest TV doctor. His audition tape was made in a bathroom in Namibia, when filming 'Flight of the Phoenix', looking unshaven and scruffy; the director thought he was perfect and had no idea that he was British. The part has gained him three Emmy nominations, two Golden Globe awards and two Screen Actors Guild awards.

Laurie has said that having to put on an American accent is "the single hardest thing … I pray that no one's going to get a coronary artery – I can say the coronary and I can say the artery, I just need about five minutes in between lying down in a dark room." Currently into its fifth series 'House' recently passed the 100th episode milestone. Back in 2004 when he went to LA to make the pilot he lived in an hotel and never unpacked because he was so worried the show wouldn't last.

He is a talented musician, playing several instruments, including the piano, and is in several celebrity rock groups which perform for charity, including 'Poor White Trash and the Little Big Horns' alongside Lenny Henry. He has written two novels: 'The Gun Seller', a best seller which has been adapted for film, and 'The Paper Soldier', due out soon.

In 1989 he married Jo Green and they have three children. Passionate about motorbikes (his children also ride them) he has a Triumph Bonneville which he rides in LA, whilst in London he has a Yamaha. He is a member of the Leander Club, one of the oldest rowing clubs in the world, and has taken up boxing. In 2007 he was appointed OBE for services to acting.

Joanna Lumley OBE
'Actress, Writer, Campaigner, Model'

How fitting that such a lovely woman was born in one of the most beautiful places in the world, Kashmir, on 1st May 1946. On both sides of her family India had been their real home for generations, and her father was a Major with the Gurkhas.

The family left India at Partition and Joanna attended schools in Hong Kong and Malaya before English boarding schools. She has written of how, before air travel, it took months to get from the Far East to England so that once she did not see her father for 1½ years. Despite this she was happy, being naturally gregarious and able to make the best of life.

She became a very successful model, and gradually found work as an actress starting with 'Some Girls Do'. In 1969 she was a Bond Girl in 'On Her Majesty's Secret Service', and in 1975 landed the role of Purdey in 'The New Avengers' opposite Patrick Macnee. For this she created the iconic 'Purdey' hairstyle, and learned kick boxing and karate. In 1979 she co-starred in 'Sapphire and Steel' opposite David McCallum. She has appeared in many films, plays and on television, but her most famous role is surely the wonderfully dreadful Patsy of 'Absolutely Fabulous'. Her documentaries and travel programmes include 'In the Kingdom of the Thunder Dragon' retracing her grandparents' journey to Bhutan in the 1930s.

Her writing includes travel books, an autobiography 'No Room for Secrets', columns for The Times and a book accompanying an Imperial War Museum exhibition. This last led her to fulfil the final wishes of Emily Chitticks whose fiancée died in WWI, and who had wanted his letters buried with her. These had been lodged with the Museum and could not be released, but it is typical of Joanna's kindness that she had them copied and laid in Emily's grave.

She is practical (installing and painting missing floorboards in her home), and bemoans the fact that in our disposable society young people are not taught to sew and cook, or change tyres and fuses (all of which she can do).

She is brave too. In a bar, noticing an armed man, who had a very large glass of whisky and looked "quite nervous", she went over and asked him why he had a gun because "It seemed sensible to engage him in some sort of talk because once you start talking people are much less likely to feel violent or exiled or hostile. So it wasn't brave, only sensible. ….. I hated it when people said ….. don't have a go. I do believe have a go."

She took up the cause of VC hero Tul Bahadar Pun. This man, a Gurkha, had saved her father's life as a chindit fighting for the British and won the Victoria Cross. When, aged 84, he was unable to obtain medical treatment in Nepal he applied to live in Britain only to be told, unbelievably, that he had "failed to demonstrate strong ties with Britain". In 2009 she continued her work on behalf of ex Gurkhas with a stunningly successful campaign which eventually won them the right to settle in Britain.

A life enhancer, she is Patron of the Born Free Foundation and works for many charities, including Comic Relief, Mind and Sight Savers. She cares deeply about the environment, "You aren't going to leave this planet ever, so keep it nice", and sponsors the Oxford Joanna Lumley Fellowship in Environmental Science. She is also a Director of Frogmat an environmental company dealing with problems of oil pollution and ground protection.

She has a son, Jamie, and two granddaughters. She first married Jeremy Lloyd, and is now married to conductor Stephen Barlow. She was appointed OBE in 1995, is a fellow of the Royal Geographical Society and holds an honorary degree from the University of St Andrews and an honorary doctorate from Queen's University, Belfast.

Jennifer Saunders
'Actress & Writer'

She was born on 6 July 1958 in Lincolnshire. Her father was an RAF pilot who once, according to Jennifer, flew upside down under telegraph wires to impress her mother. Growing up in an RAF family she spent much of her childhood moving, and attended various schools (often joining mid-term) which made her extremely observant of other people and how to fit in without being noticed.

She joined the Central School of Speech and Drama studying to become a drama teacher. On the same course was Dawn French. They didn't hit it off straight away - Jennifer once said Dawn was "terribly, terribly bouncy" whilst she was "vaguely rigid and introverted" (although she puts her stiff upper lip down to flute playing rather than inbreeding). They eventually shared a flat with several others. Dawn was organised and tidy, but Jennifer was so disorganised and untidy that once, after a burglary, when the police reported that Jennifer's room had been particularly badly hit, it turned out that the burglars hadn't touched it! Today she is extremely tidy and cites sweeping as a very helpful aid to writing.

They started working together, initially performing to family and friends. Then they saw an advert for London's Comic Strip which was looking for new talent. They applied and were accepted (later claiming this was because there were few female comics and they at least had breasts). They appeared on television in 'The Comic Strip Presents', a series that started with 'Five Go Mad in Dorset'. Next was 'Girls on Top' which Jennifer co-wrote, and then in 1987 came the first of the hugely successful 'French and Saunders' series which ran for 20 years. French and Saunders took their act on tour in the UK, most recently in what is, sadly, possibly their final tour 'French and Saunders Still Alive: 2008'.

Jennifer is equally famous for writing and staring in the BAFTA and Emmy award winning series 'Absolutely Fabulous'. It came from a sketch she had written for 'French and Saunders', but because Dawn was adopting a baby and needed time out

Jennifer developed it solo. It ran for five series and her Ab Fab co-star, Joanna Lumley, has highlighted Jennifer's gift as a writer for linking the development of a character over several series with the way the actor is portraying it. Later television work includes 'Jam and Jerusalem' and 'The Life and Times of Vivienne Vyle'.

In 2005 Jennifer won the People's Choice Award for Favourite Movie Villain as the voice of the Fairy Godmother in 'Shrek 2' - despite the character's demise she had the line "I'll be back" recorded just in case. She has won a Writers' Guild of Great Britain Award and, in 1992, a BAFTA for 'Absolutely Fabulous'. In 2009 she and Dawn French were awarded a BAFTA Fellowship. In 2007 she received an Honorary Doctorate of Literature from Exeter University. In 2001 she declined an OBE.

She married fellow performer, Adrian Edmondson, in 1985. Living mainly in Devon their three daughters didn't realise they had famous parents for quite a while. When she appeared on 'Top Gear' ("because my kids just love the show I finally gave in") she revealed herself as "a very, very competitive person" and produced the fastest lap by a woman - 1.46.1. She has always loved cars, her first being an Alfa Romeo Spider, the first of three Alfa Romeos she's owned; Clarkson was impressed.

Invited to receive an award at the LGBT Awards in New York Saunders and Lumley arrived as Edina and Patsy, dressed outrageously even by their standards, only to find it was a serious black suited affair with Senators present, and long, meaningful speeches. All Jennifer had prepared, after her 6th glass of champagne on the flight over, was "Cheers, Thanks a lot" which she duly delivered, "the worst, most embarrassing moment of my life".

Renée Zellweger
'Bridget Jones and many others'

Although a bit of a tomboy, following her elder brother, Drew, around everywhere, including joining the Drama Club at school, it was not until her role as Dorothy, opposite Tom Cruise, in 'Jerry Maguire' (1996) that she was catapulted to fame. Renée Kathleen Zellweger was born on 25 April 1969 in Texas. Her father, Emil, is a Swiss electrical engineer in the oil industry and her mother, Kjellfried Irene, a midwife, is descended from the Sami people of Norway.

She attended James Bowie Elementary and Stephen F Austin Elementary until fourth grade when, aged 9, the family moved to Katy, a suburb of Texas, where she went to Katy High School. Here the family built a house from scratch. Her father taught her to be very practical, teaching her how to change a tyre and fix the brakes on a car but more importantly she helped wire the house, dig the septic system and tile the floors and walls; all very useful in helping with her very convincing performance as the practical Ruby in 'Cold Mountain'.

On leaving school in 1987 she went to the University of Texas in Austin to major in English Language. She took drama classes to fulfil a Fine Arts requirement which reinforced the joy of acting. During her time at university she supported herself by waitressing, and graduated in 1991 with a BA degree in English.

Instead of heading for LA and Hollywood she decided to stay in Texas and pursue an acting career there. She played small roles in films such as 'A Taste for Killing' (1992), 'Murder in the Heartland' (1993) and 'Reality Bites' (1994). Her first debut lead role was in a film called 'In Love and a .45' (1994) for which she was nominated Best Debut Performance at the Independent Spirit Awards. She then played in 'The Return of the Texas Chainsaw Massacre' (1994) before landing the starring role in 'The Whole Wide World' (1996).

Her film career took off and in 2001 she was awarded her first Golden Globe award for her role in 'Nurse Betty' (2000). She went on to star in 'Me, Myself & Irene' (2000) alongside Jim Carrey, 'Bridget Jones's Diary' (2001), with Hugh Grant and Colin Firth, for which she was nominated for an Academy Award, and as Roxie Hart in 'Chicago' (2002). This role earned her a second Golden Globe award and an Oscar nomination, a fine feat for someone who had no previous singing or dancing experience prior to filming.

In 2003 she played in 'Cold Mountain' and was awarded her third Golden Globe, an Oscar and a BAFTA for Best Supporting Actress. She has also starred in the sequel 'Bridget Jones: The Edge of Reason' (2004), 'Cinderella Man' (2004) and 'Miss Potter' (2006). In 2007 she appeared in 'Leatherheads' and the following year, 'Appaloosa'. Others that have been released in 2009 or are due for release include 'Case 39', 'My One and Only', 'Chilled in Miami', 'My Own Love Song', 'New in Town' and 'Monsters vs Aliens'. She has also lent her voice in 'Shark Tale' (2003), as Angie the Angel fish and in 'Bee Movie' (2007) as Vanessa Bloom.

She has been a guest on many television chat shows including 'The Tonight Show with Jay Leno', and 'The Late Show with David Letterman', 'Parkinson' and 'Friday Night with Jonathan Ross'.

She married singer Kenny Chesney in May 2005 but this did not work out and the marriage was annulled in December of the same year.

She has won and been nominated for many awards from Best Breakthrough Performer to Best Actress, and in 2005 she was awarded a star on the Hollywood Walk of Fame.

THE TAILOR OF GLOUCESTER
MRS TITTLE-MOUSE
SQUIRREL NUTKIN
TOM KITTEN
PETER RABBIT
Lucy.

Cilla Black OBE
'Singer, TV Superstar & "a lorra, lorra, laughs"'

Priscilla White was born in Liverpool on 27th May 1943. Her Irish father was a docker and the family lived in a flat over a shop. Her extremely happy childhood was full of music with her father and brothers playing musical instruments and her mother singing. There was a piano in the flat and friends and neighbours congregated here for a singsong when the pubs closed. Cilla would sit on the stairs, longing to perform. When she was five her chance came and on the kitchen table in her nightdress she sang an Al Jolson number. Standing there with everyone's eyes on her she was in her element; in her autobiography 'What's It All About?' she recalls it as "the most marvellous feeling in the whole world."

Her mother, who ran a market stall selling second hand clothes, brought her children up as staunch Roman Catholics - as a child Cilla feared for her soul when she realised she had eaten half an orange flavoured with an Oxo cube on a Friday.

Cilla was a tomboy and nearly killed herself jumping off the back of a fast moving lorry. She also suffered a broken nose which needed plastic surgery. At school the urge to entertain continued, and she was always playing jokes and making friends laugh. To her parents' delight her last report read "Priscilla is suitable for office work" – Cilla wanted "suitable for stardom"!

Music was her passion. She became friends with Ringo Starr, and idolised Cliff Richard, blowing a week's wages on a taxi to follow what she thought was his car. She started doing numbers with local bands, becoming so popular that when the Beatles played John Lennon had to ask 'Cyril' to sing with them. At the Cavern Club she wangled a job taking coats, and she was a waitress at the Zodiac Club where, aged 17, she met one Bobby Willis.

By then billed as 'Swinging Priscilla', the Beatles persuaded their manager, Brian Epstein, to audition Cilla with their backing. It was a disaster – she was terrified and they played in a different key to the one she sang in. Happily, he later caught her singing when she had no idea he was in and signed her – his only female artist. As she was under 21 Cilla's dad had to sign the contract, something he initially refused to do when he saw her name had been changed to Cilla Black (the result of an earlier misprint).

After success on 'Ready, Steady, Go!' Cilla quit work to audition for EMI's George Martin (again her father took some persuading). He gave her a contract and in 1963 her first single, Lennon & MCartney's 'Love of the Loved', started a highly successful, long lasting recording career. Her next single, 'Anyone Who Had a Heart' (until 2009 the best selling single ever by a British female artist) reached No 1, followed by another No 1, 'You're My World'. During the 60s she had 20 consecutive Top 40 hits.

In 1967 Epstein secured a TV series starring Cilla. Her television career went from strength to strength and she became the highest paid female performer on British television, eventually hosting 'Surprise, Surprise' and 'Blind Date'. She has worked phenomenally hard with endless tours, summer seasons, pantomimes, records and shows and never lets audiences down (even performing when one of her sons was desperately ill). "If you're lucky enough to have an audience, if you live a good life thanks to that audience, then you have a commitment – a job to do."

In 1997 she was appointed OBE, and in 2000 received an Honorary Fellowship from Liverpool John Moores University. The man she had met at the Zodiac Club really was the only one for her and in 1969 she married Bobby Willis who had become her manager. They were very happy until his death from cancer in 1999. They had four children, 3 sons and a baby daughter, Ellen, who was born prematurely and died shortly after birth. In 2004 Cilla became a grandmother. She has homes in Buckinghamshire, London, Spain and Barbados.

Alfred Brendel Hon KBE
'Pianist and Writer'

According to his website, one of the world's greatest musicians, Alfred Brendel, wasn't a child prodigy, his parents weren't musicians and there was no music in the house. He also says he doesn't have a phenomenal memory and is not a good sight reader. Nevertheless, during his 60 year career his name became one that guaranteed a performance would be sold out.

He has mixed German, Austrian, Italian and Slav ancestry and was born on 31st January 1931 in Wiesenberg, northern Moravia (now the Czech Republic). His father's occupations included hotel manager, which is where Brendel first heard "more elevated" music when he played records for guests on a wind up gramophone. When he was 6 he had his first piano lessons, and later attended Graz Conservatory. However, by the age of 16, apart from a few master classes, he had finished his formal musical education; something he regards as an advantage because it meant he had to work things out for himself, listening to other musicians and remaining uninfluenced by teachers.

In Graz, aged 17, he simultaneously staged his first public recital, 'The Fugue in Piano Literature', and exhibited his watercolours in a local gallery. A year later he won 4th prize in the prestigious Busoni Piano Competition, launching his career. It was a slow, step by step, progression until he gave a performance in London with a programme he says he did not particularly like, yet the next day three recording companies offered him contracts.

He was the first pianist ever to record the entire piano works of Beethoven and is one of the few to have recorded all Mozart's piano concertos. His discography covers solo and orchestral works ranging from Bach and Haydn to Weber, Schubert, Schumann, Liszt, Brahms, Mussorgsky, and Schoenberg.

Asked how much of his success he would put down to talent and how much to hard work he said talent is only one ingredient, citing also the need to be healthy and the importance of luck, patience, perseverance, memory and good nerves (which he commented wryly "you will also sometimes need when you read the newspaper") – and finally, rather than hard work, the ability to do "what was necessary with full concentration".

His extra-musical interests range from Romanesque architecture to Dada, Shakespeare and nonsense verse, amongst others. Listing "laughing" as a favourite occupation he famously gave a Darwin Lecture entitled 'Does Classical Music have to be entirely serious?' He is fascinated by the grotesque and traces his love of the absurd back to a little song from the Berlin of the 1920s that his mother sometimes sang to him starting "I tear out one of my eyelashes and stab you dead with it … ". His twin passions are words and music and he has had several volumes of poems published. He now concentrates on his profession as a writer.

In 2008 he gave his final concert with a performance of Mozart's 9th Piano Concerto. In an interview he recalled with a characteristic twinkle how a sore throat almost saw a colleague having to undertake this final performance - one can only imagine the understudy's feelings! Fortunately antibiotics worked and Brendel said "I took away a feeling of warmth and gratitude which will stay with me, but I did not shed a tear". He chose not to have this last concert filmed, explaining that he finds cameras too stressful, so only a lucky few heard that last wonderful performance.

Since 1971 he and his wife, Irene, have lived in London; they have a son, Adrian (a cellist) and two daughters. He has one daughter by his first marriage. His countless musical prizes and awards include the Hans von Bilow medal of the Berlin Philharmonic and honorary membership of the Wiener Philharmoniker. He has honorary degrees from Oxford and Yale, and in 1989 was awarded an Honorary KBE.

Sir James Galway OBE
'The Man with the Golden Flute'

The world's greatest flute player; which is not surprising since his father, grandfather and great-grandfather had all been flute players and his mother was a self-taught pianist. He was born on 8 December 1939 in Northern Ireland and in the Irish community at that time if you did not play an instrument, you sang.

He started with a mouth organ, quickly mastering this he moved on to one with a button on the side allowing him to play half-tones. Next was a penny-whistle and by the age of 7 began playing the violin he had been given by a neighbour. He did not enjoy it and took up the flute, playing his father's, even after it had been taken apart and hidden around the house.

Although academic he did not like to study, he just wanted to play. In 1949, aged 10, he won all three classes in the Irish Flute Championships; he had entered all three age categories even though he was only eligible for two.

On leaving school he tried to get a job as an apprentice book binder but was turned down and ended up working in a piano shop, which he did not enjoy and was often found sleeping under the pianos rather than repairing them. At one point he found himself playing for the 39th Old Boys on Tuesdays and Fridays, the Youth Orchestra on Saturdays, the Studio Orchestra on Wednesdays, delivering newspapers in the evening and working in the piano shop during the day. In his spare time he took lessons and practiced; an exhausting schedule even for a 14 year old boy.

At the age of 15 he studied at the Royal College of Music in London for three years and while there became a member of the London Junior Orchestra, and also played with the Morley College Orchestra. He earned a scholarship to study at the Guildhall School of Music for a year and later a scholarship at the Paris Conservatoire; which he quit after eight months.

At 21 he worked with the Saddler's Wells Orchestra, with a short break when he joined the Royal Opera House, returning after a season to play Saddlers Wells with his lifelong friend the oboist Derek Wickens. He obtained a job with the BBC Symphony Orchestra but a few weeks later he received an invitation to play with the London Symphony Orchestra as first flute, a dream come true. He later joined the Royal Philharmonic Orchestra before successfully auditioning for the Berlin Philharmonic Orchestra under Herbert von Karajan, becoming principal flute in 1969. However, in 1975, to Karajan's surprise, he decided that he would leave to pursue a solo career. Since then, in addition to playing at numerous concerts throughout the world, he has recorded over 60 CDs with Sony Classics, a new range of CDs with Deutsche Gramophone and sold over 30 million albums.

In 1977, while living in Switzerland, he was run over by a speeding motorbike. He sustained a broken arm and broken legs, and was put in traction. He endured a major operation to reset and repair splintered and broken bones and spent months in hospital and then in a wheelchair before he could walk again. During this time it never occurred to him that he would not play the flute again.

He has been married three times. Firstly to Claire LeBastard; they had one son. Secondly, in 1972 he married Anna Renggli; they had a son and twin daughters. In 1978 he recorded the instrumental version of John Denver's 'Annie's Song' for her. In 1984 he married, Jeanne Cinante.

He was appointed OBE in 1977 and knighted in 2001. He was Musician of the Year in 1997 and in 2004 was given the President's Merit Award from the Recording Academy at the Grammy's 8th Annual 'Salute to Classical Music'. In 2005 he received the 'Outstanding Contribution to Classical Music' award.

Kylie Minogue OBE
'She Puts the 'Show' into Show Business'

It has been an extraordinary transformation from Charlene, the squeaky clean, girl next door of long running soap, 'Neighbours', to Kylie, the internationally famous singer with record sales of over 60 million, and sultry star of a raunchy advert for Agent Provocateur. Throughout the transformation Kylie's essential charm, self-deprecating humour and love of life have shone through, coupled with a steely determination to succeed no matter how hard she has to work. Born in Melbourne, Australia on 28th May 1968 her mother, a former ballerina, encouraged her children's showbiz careers. From Kylie's father, an accountant, came financial acumen as he guided the management of her fortune. Kylie remains extremely close to her family and her mother often accompanies her on tours.

By the time she was 12 Kylie was playing parts in soap operas. At 16 a role in 'The Henderson Kids' brought her money which she spent on singing lessons and making a demo cassette because she figured it might be useful if a director wanted an actress who could sing a bit. Originally her younger sister, Dannii, had the more successful career and Kylie had to forge Dannii's signature on photos for her fans. But in 1986 Kylie was cast as Charlene in 'Neighbours'. Her on screen romance with co-star Jason Donovan caught the imagination of the public and the wedding episode in 1987 attracted over 20 million viewers.

In 1987 her single 'Locomotion' reached No 1 in Australia. A meeting was arranged with Pete Waterman of Stock, Aitken & Waterman to help her break into the UK market. Pete forgot all about it until he was told Kylie had arrived in the UK and was sitting in reception demanding to see him. He famously remarked "She should be so lucky". She had to wait over an hour but it was worth it - Stock, Aitken and Waterman wrote 'I Should Be So Lucky' for her which reached No 1 in 12 countries, including the first simultaneous No 1 in Australia and Britain. In 1993 she signed with deConstruction focusing on more cutting

edge work. In 1999 she changed direction again, signing with Parlaphone. Her phenomenally successful career has spanned over 20 years, with fantastic stage shows, costumes and videos. She was paid £250,000 to perform at the wedding of Vanisha, daughter of steel magnate Lakshmi Mittal.

An accomplished seamstress she can make her own clothes. Despite her love of designer clothes she also buys second hand – famously paying 50p for the gold hot pants she wore in the 'Spinning Around' video.

She continues to act and played the Absinthe Fairy in 'Moulin Rouge'. She also appeared with David Tennant in 'Dr Who' in 2007. In 2000 she performed before millions at the Sydney Olympics Closing Ceremony, and for the opening of the Paralympics. She is an icon of the gay community and has appeared at the Sydney Gay and Lesbian Mardi Gras.

She has had many romances and her love life is closely scrutinised by the press. The on screen romance with 'Neighbours' co-star, Jason Donovan, was true in real life, and there was consternation when it was followed by a seemingly unlikely affair with INXS star, Michael Hutchence. But it was serious and Kylie was devastated when it ended. Other beaux have included French actor, Olivier Martinez.

In May 2005, during her 'Showgirl' tour and just short of her 37th birthday, she was diagnosed with breast cancer. Eighteen months later, with the cancer in remission, she was back with the 'Showgirl Homecoming' tour which opened in Australia. In 2007 the V&A staged 'Kylie – The Exhibition'.

In 2008 she was appointed OBE for services to music, and the French government made her a Chevalier des Arts et des Lettres for her contribution to the enrichment of French culture. She is an ambassador for the NSPCC.

Gordon Sumner CBE
'Sting'

It's the early 1970s and the bass player has turned up wearing a black and yellow striped top – "Sting" quips a band member. The nickname stuck but it took years of playing gigs in the UK and US (courtesy of economy flights on Freddie Laker's Skytrain) before it was the name of an international rock star.

Born a Geordie on 2nd October 1951 Sting was the eldest of four. His father had a milk round which Sting helped on. His father loved his mother all his life but she loved another man, remaining torn between him and her family until she eloped. Divorce wasn't an option and Sting grew up in an atmosphere of domestic unhappiness. His grandmother, Agnes, who left school at 14, had a love of books which she encouraged in him. She read the Reader's Digest, explaining she needed short cuts as she hadn't had a proper education, and completed The Times crossword every day. Sting was brought up a Roman Catholic but had problems with confession since he didn't think he'd done anything wrong. Instead he made up sins - a sin he didn't dare confess – "thought and torment seem to be inextricably linked and this is the lasting legacy of my Catholicism".

There was music at home, whether it was his father singing or his mother playing the piano, and a great-uncle was mentioned in dispatches for playing the accordion under fire as he "kept up the morale of the troops in the most trying of circumstances". Another uncle emigrated leaving a worn out acoustic guitar which Sting pounced on "like a starving man in a cake shop".

He won a scholarship to St Cuthbert's Grammar School, Newcastle where his teachers inspired him to learn. Looking for something that would give him time to develop his musical ambitions he obtained a student grant and enrolled at teacher training college. Here he met another ex-grammar school boy desperate to break into music and they formed 'Last Exit'. Whilst working with the band Sting was contacted by Sister Ruth, head of St

Paul's First School, Cramlington. She had taught Sting's sister and seeing he was qualified to teach invited him for an interview. A look at his bank balance convinced him to attend and he became the teacher of 30 lucky eight-year olds.

Every Wednesday 'Last Exit' played at Gosforth. Noticing attractive girls arriving for the gigs Sting practiced "piercing and hopefully smouldering glances from the stage". After a booking on a cruise ship Sting vowed the next time he sang on a boat it would belong to him. In 1977, Sting, his wife, Frances, their baby son and the dog set off for London with no home, jobs or money, just a phone number for one Stewart Copeland, with whom he would form 'The Police' - a massively successful rock band which has sold over 50 million records and won endless platinum discs and awards. Their 1983 No 1 single, 'Every Breath You Take', is still one of the most played records on American radio. 'The Police' broke up in 1984 but reformed in 2007 for tours which sell out famous venues worldwide.

In 1985 Sting embarked on a hugely successful solo career, which has included acting. In 2006, inspired by the work of the 16th Century lutenist and composer, John Dowland, he released 'Songs From The Labyrinth' which topped classical music charts and quadrupled lute sales worldwide. In 2003 he published 'Broken Music – A Memoir'.

A member of Amnesty International Sting is an environmental and humanitarian campaigner. He founded the Rainforest Foundation, and a Colombian tree frog, Dendropsophus stingi, was named for him. Sting and Frances divorced in 1984. In 1992 he married Trudie Styler with whom he has four children. His homes in Europe and the States include an Elizabethan manor house in Wiltshire. In 2002 he was appointed CBE and in 2006 was awarded an Honorary Doctorate of Music by Newcastle University.

Colonel John Blashford-Snell OBE
'The Original Indiana Jones'

He was born on 22 October 1936 in Hereford. His father, 'Bish', was a Rector and a leading figure in local affairs. His mother, Gwen, had a love of animals and would nurse them back to health which meant he was raised surrounded by horses, cows, cats, dogs, rabbits, tortoises, parrots and even a monkey.

As a boy he loved building things, blowing them up and finding ways of crossing obstacles; after the war he would dig up German land mines in Jersey and throw them off the cliffs. His sense of adventure had been kindled with the Boy Scouts; his parents spent much time leading and helping the local Scout and Guide troops.

His was educated at Victoria College, Jersey and spent most of the school holidays with the TA, his father being chaplain of a gunner regiment in Monmouthshire.

In 1956 he entered the Royal Military Academy, Sandhurst and was commissioned into the Royal Engineers; he served 37 years in the Army, retiring in 1991. In 1958 he was posted to a Squadron based in Cyprus and ran the Underwater Section. In 1962 he was posted back to Sandhurst and became the Adventure Training Officer.

He has led over 100 expeditions to some of the remotest parts of the world. He has taken dentists, doctors and eye specialists along to help previously undiscovered cities and tribes. His expeditions are some of the most dangerous, challenging and fulfilling known to man. He has seen and overcome every possible obstacle, be it desert, swamp, or jungle; looked adversity in the face, and has hacked, swum, dug and paddled his way back to civilisation.

In 1968 he was selected to lead an Army/civilian team to explore and make the first descent of the infamous Blue Nile; this expedition effectively launched white-water rafting as a sport. In 1971 he led the expedition of the first vehicle crossing of the Darien Gap and in 1974 navigated almost all (there are some waterfalls!) 2,700 miles of the great Zaire (now Congo) River.

Inspired by Sir Frances Drake and encouraged by Prince Charles he set up 'Operation Drake' which, between 1978 and 1980, organised projects for young people from 27 nations working with scientists and servicemen in 16 countries. In 1984 'Operation Raleigh' was launched and by 1992 over 10,000 young people from 50 nations had taken part in challenges and global expeditions, returning home true young pioneers. Later his teams went on to discover and protect a giant elephant, thought to be a mammoth, in Nepal.

In 1993 he became Chairman of a £2.5m appeal to establish a centre which would provide vocational training and guidance for the youth of Merseyside. He later helped set up the Liverpool Construction Crafts Guild to promote training of skilled craftsmen.

In 2000, to encourage a remote tribe to remain in the forest, he took a grand piano through jungle and up rivers for the musical Wai Wai tribe in Guyana. In 2005 he discovered an abandoned 19th-century submarine off Panama and in 2006 his teams sailed to a remote island off Chilean Patagonia in search of the HMS Wager, a British ship lost in 1741, and found its wreckage. He has also pioneered the use of paramotors in scientific expeditions.

He married Judith in 1960; they have two daughters, Victoria and Emma. He has been awarded the Segrave Trophy, the Livingstone Medal and in 1993 was presented with the Royal Geographical Society's Patrons Medal for the encouragement of exploration for young people. In 1994 he was awarded the Institute of Royal Engineers' Gold Medal, and was appointed MBE in 1969 and OBE in 1996.

Today he concentrates on helping disadvantaged youngsters in Britain's concrete jungle and people in need in remote green jungles.

Sir Ranulph Fiennes OBE

'World's Greatest Living Explorer' (Guiness Book of Records)

Ranulph Twisleton-Wykeham-Fiennes, so named after his father, was born on 7 March 1944 in Sunningdale. Ranulph never met his father as he had died from injuries received in WWII, four months before Ran was born.

After living in South Africa, where his grandmother's family were based, the family returned to England in 1954. From Sandroyd Prep School, he scraped into Eton, where he joined the College Corps; he had always wanted to be commanding officer of the Royal Scots Greys, like his father. He did not relish his time at Eton until his last 18 months when he and a friend started to climb buildings at night – he did not climb in daylight due to his vertigo. He left Eton early to enrol at a crammer in Hove enabling him to gain his fifth 'O' Level; needed to ensure his acceptance at Mons Officer Cadet School. In 1963, he joined the Royal Scots Greys in Germany.

He joined 22 SAS but was expelled during training because of the 'Castle Combe' affair, involving a trout stream, explosives and the filming of 'The Adventures of Dr Doolittle'. He rejoined the RSG but soon volunteered to serve out his last two years of service in Oman where he was awarded the Dhofar Campaign Medal and the Sultan's Bravery Medal. On leaving the Regular Army he joined 21st SAS (Territorial) Regiment.

After the army he decided he would lecture and write for half the year and lead sponsored expeditions the other half. Some of his expeditions include: the Fabergstolsbre Glacier and the then unclimbed Briksdalsbre Glacier in Norway; the first recorded north to south trans-navigation of British Columbia in 1971, the route was along nine interconnecting waterways, some of the roughest and fastest rivers in the world; the first surface journey around the world's axis, 'Transglobe', between 1979 and 1982 making him and Charlie Burton the first men in history to reach both Poles; the South Pole on 15 December 1980 and the North Pole on 10 April 1982.

In 1991/2 he went with Dr Mike Stroud on an unsupported expedition to the South Pole reaching the Pole on 16 January 1992. However, to complete the expedition, with 289 nautical miles to go, they had to radio for pick up. This was still the first crossing of the Antarctic continent and the longest polar journey in history (1,350 miles). In 2003, three months after a heart attack and double bypass, he completed the Land Rover 7x7x7 challenge; 7 marathons in 7 days in 7 continents.

In 2005 he attempted to climb Everest, making it to 'Death Camp' before having to return with heart problems. In 2008 he tried again, but had to turn back. In 2009, at the third attempt, he reached the summit, becoming the oldest Briton and first British pensioner to achieve this. In 2007 he climbed the North Face of The Eiger.

Well known for his expeditions, he has travelled to the most dangerous and inaccessible parts on earth, has faced death on many occasions, cut off his own frostbitten fingers with a fretsaw, suffered snow blindness and gangrene, has seen ice-packs explode within feet of him and has fallen into crevasses, the list is endless. He has run countless marathons and taken part in many endurance races, mostly to ensure that he will be in shape for his tortuous expeditions.

He married, Virginia 'Ginny' Pepper, his childhood sweetheart, in 1970. She died of stomach cancer in 2004. In 2005 he married Louise Millington; they have a daughter, Elizabeth, born in 2006.

He inherited his father's Baronetcy at birth but in his own right has received many awards and was appointed OBE in 1993. He has received numerous honorary degrees and was nominated Great British Sportsman of the Year in 2007, aged 63.

He has raised over £12 million for charity, his aim is to raise £15 million before he dies. He has published numerous books about his and other great explorers' travels and expeditions.

Martina Milburn
'The Prince's Trust'

Appointed Chief Executive of the Prince's Trust, in May 2004, she is responsible for developing the strategic direction of the Trust, and sits on the Trust's trading board overseeing 700 staff and 8,500 volunteers. The Trust was established by HRH The Prince of Wales in 1976 and has to date assisted over 575,000 young people, having an annual turnover in excess of £50 million.

She was born on 5th September 1957, the eldest of five sisters; educated at the Mater Dei School for Girls, a Roman Catholic School in Welwyn Garden City. Her parents did a great deal of work for charity and this clearly has had an influence in the direction of her working life. She started work in 1976 in the Press Association as the first female reporter on a junior journalists training scheme, previously restricted to men. She worked in TV, radio and also freelance for a number of charities including the Catholic Fund for Overseas Development.

In 1993 she was appointed Chief Executive of the Association of Spinal Injury Research, Rehabilitation and Reintegration (ASPIRE) which is a charity whose purpose is to help with the rehabilitation of those who have a spinal injury. Whilst there, she was responsible for bringing in the ASPIRE National Training Centre on time and on budget and helping to turn round the fortunes of the charity. When she started, there were five staff but by the time she left, seven years later, there were 100.

In 2000 she became chief executive of the BBC Children in Need Appeal where, during her tenure, she helped raise over £100 million, laying the foundations for the doubling of its income and capturing a bigger television audience.

Four years later she was appointed Chief Executive of the Prince's Trust the purpose of which is to encourage young people to take responsibility for themselves – helping them build the life they choose rather than the one they've ended up with.

In the UK today one in five young people are not in work, education or training. Youth unemployment costs the UK economy £10 million a day in lost productivity, while youth crime costs £1 billion every year.

The Trust gives practical and financial support to the young people who need it most, helping them develop key skills, confidence and motivation, which enables them to move into work, education or training.

About a quarter of those being assisted by the Trust have committed offences but she says, "Some of them go on to become very successful business people. My personal view is that if you are a successful drug dealer you have actually got good entrepreneurial skills. It's just that drugs are never going to give you a future. What we can offer is a legitimate path to a decent future." She goes on to say "we have a 12 week personal development programme that makes the most enormous difference to people's lives. Meet them on week one and they won't talk to each other. By the end of week 12 they have confidence and believe in themselves. Very often they say it's the first time that anyone has believed in them."

She is frustrated, at times, when she has to turn people needing assistance away because there are insufficient funds and, in the current financial climate, raising funds is more challenging than ever. She says "It's not that people are saying 'we are not going to give you any money'. They're saying 'we are not going to give you any money at the moment. We still want to support you. We hope in six months time we will give you what we promised'."

She is married to Keith; they have three sons, Matthew, Daniel and Samuel.

Prince's Trust

Charlie Dimmock
'The Botticelli Garden Venus'

Charlotte Elouise Dimmock was born on 10 August 1966 in Hampshire to Terry, a merchant seaman, and Sue, a beautiful bohemian mother. When Charlie was 16 her parents divorced but it was amicable and they remained friends with Charlie being close to both of them. Tragically she lost her mother and stepfather in the 2004 Asian Tsunami.

She has described an extremely happy childhood living on the edge of the New Forest where she spent a lot of time outdoors, either helping her grandfather in his garden, or playing in the forest. As a teenager she had a Saturday job at Mill Water Gardens which sparked her interest in gardening as a career; it was also here that she developed her passion for horticultural water features. She started 'A' levels but dropped out, and eventually went on to study horticulture, gaining a distinction in a BTEC Diploma in Amenity Horticulture and a National Technical Certificate in Turfculture and Sporting Management. As part of her training she spent a year at the Chelsea Physic Garden.

She saved her wages and travelled in New Zealand (where she reputedly had a stint as an Air NZ check-in clerk complete with strict dress code), Australia, Fiji and the Cook Islands. Back in the UK she worked at Mill Water Gardens as manager. It was here, in 1992, that researchers from Meridian TV came wanting to film someone putting in a pond for an episode of 'Grass Roots'. Charlie said she could only sell them the equipment. The researchers were desperate to film someone doing the work and eventually Charlie agreed to do it on her day off. That resulting three minute feature was part of a programme directed by John Thornicroft who, five years later, when he wanted a female presenter for 'Ground Force', remembered Charlie.

'Ground Force' was a phenomenal success with fourteen series running over eight years, and an American version. The banter between the presenters and Charlie's natural enthusiasm and equally natural (and braless) appearance sparked 8 million viewers.

Other TV work has included 'Garden Invaders' (2003); 'Garden for all Seasons UK Style' (2003); 'Cheer for Charlie' (2002) when she became a trapeze artist; 'Charlie and the Duchess' (2001/2); 'Charlie's Gardening Neighbours' (BBC); 'Girls on Top' (2001) in which she tried a variety of jobs; 'Charlie's Wildlife Gardens' (2000); 'Charlie's Garden Army' (1999/2000) and American CBS' 'The Early Show'. She has also presented the Chelsea and Hampton Court Palace Flower Shows, and made guest appearances on 'Ready, Steady, Cook' and 'The Kumars at No 42'. Her series 'River Walks' on UKTV charting the history, wildlife, recreation and industries of the rivers of Southern England began its third series in 2008. She has written gardening and water feature books, including 'Enjoy Your Own Garden'.

She does a great deal for charity, internationally and locally, to raise funds for organisations such as the Cystic Fibrosis Trust (the Growing Hope Rose was created to raise awareness of CF and funds for the CF Trust, and was launched by Charlie at Hampton Court), Breakthrough Breast Cancer (for which she walked the Great Wall of China) and Delta (which helps deaf children). She is a Patron of Dream Flight a charity giving severely sick and disabled children the holiday of a lifetime in Florida's theme parks, and she supports conservation charities. In 2002 she ran the London Marathon (when she considered wearing a t-shirt printed with "I have got a bra on") and climbed Kilimanjaro on behalf of the Guerba/Village Education Project.

For a TV star she is unique in not possessing a television set, when her old one stopped working she didn't bother to replace it. In an interview she summed up her philosophy as "Enjoy what you do. You spend most of your time working so if you don't enjoy it you should try something else."

Tony Hart
' "If You can Write You can Draw" '

Many people recognise Tony's most famous piece of work, but have no idea that he was the artist. It's the 'Blue Peter' ship logo which he designed for a flat fee of £100 – as he once remarked he would have preferred the BBC to pay him 1d every time it was shown.

He was born in Maidstone on October 15th 1925. His parents were interested in the arts, although his father had been discouraged from pursuing artistic ambitions by his family. He was a local government official and told his son never to work in an office - advice Hart took seriously. He left school in 1944 and joined the 1st Gurkha Rifles, serving in India where he saw wonderful colours and shapes.

Returning home he attended Maidstone College of Art and was then briefly employed as a display artist in a London store. He went freelance, and early work included painting murals in restaurants in return for meals. Then in 1952 during an interview over lunch with a BBC producer, he was asked to draw a fish – the swiftness and deftness of the illustration, produced on a paper napkin, ensured a contract. It was the start of 50 years in television where his talent and inexhaustible fund of ideas for creating art, and having fun, using anything from pasta to spray paint or motorcycle wheel-tracks, inspired generations of children to be creative.

He never patronised or dictated but inspired his viewers to try for themselves: "Show them don't tell them." He seemed to be able to portray anything, using anything, from the delicate and detailed to an elephant painted in whitewash using a pitch marker on a runway. He was always ready to try new media and relished the advent of the marker pen and, much later, digital art (admitting he needed children to help him with this).

His innovative series 'Vision On', originally designed for deaf children, ran for over ten years, stretching the imagination of children with little

hearing and those with perfect hearing, alike. "The Gallery", a wall displaying viewers' work, was born here – with the show receiving over 6,000 submissions a week, many of which were displayed to the accompaniment of 'Leftbank2' – a melody that evokes childhood instantly for many adults.

His next series, the BAFTA winning 'Take Hart', saw Tony hosting solo, and the first appearance of 'Morph' – the early plastercine creation of Sproxton and Lord (who went on to fame and fortune with 'Wallace and Grommit'). After Tony died 200 little, individual Morphs were created and exhibited at Tate Modern in a competition in his memory.

'Take Hart' was followed by 'Hart Beat', which retained "The Gallery". Tony was 69 when the series came to an end but he carried on working at the BBC for several more years. In 1998 he was awarded a BAFTA Lifetime Achievement Award for his services to children's television. In 2000 he semi-retired to concentrate on charity work, including charity auctions - a number of his pictures were auctioned for the Gurkha Welfare Trust raising "substantial" amounts.

Tragically two strokes robbed him of the use of his hands and he could no longer draw: "the greatest cross that I have to bear", but he derived enormous comfort from the fan mail he received telling him how he had inspired thousands of children to work in art. He met his wife, Jean, at the BBC, and they had a daughter and two grandchildren. Jean died in 2003 and Tony in January 2009.

The love and esteem Tony evoked is best summed up by Peter Lord "Tony Hart was a terrific artist – skilful, fluent and endlessly inventive... I think of him primarily as a communicator... effortlessly encouraging young people to express themselves in every sort of visual medium... In person, he was amazingly modest about his talent and his achievements; and that TV manner – gentlemanly, kindly, and polite – was absolutely genuine and a reflection of the man."

Clive James

'Critic, Poet, TV Presenter, Broadcaster and Author'

Originally named Vivian, after a member of the 1938 Davis Cup team, he changed it early on to Clive. He was born on 7 October 1939 in Kogarah, Sydney, Australia just as his father, wanting to do his bit during WWII, joined up. Clive never saw him again; cruelly, having survived as a Jap POW he was killed when the aircraft transporting him home crashed.

During the war he and his mother lived with his aunt in Jannali, returning to Kogarah afterwards. As a young boy he built a network of tunnels in his backyard which became a club for local boys, membership of which was highly sought after. His obsession with reading began early with Biggles, Bulldog Drummond, The Saint, Sherlock Holmes and Hornblower. He attended local junior schools and then Sydney Technical High School, where it became clear that a planned career as an engineer was untenable. He went on to Sydney University becoming literary editor of the student newspaper and directing the Union Revue.

He worked for the Sydney Morning Herald and then, aged 21, travelled to England, and obtained a place at Cambridge to read English Literature. Here he wrote for university magazines and became President of the Footlights. His writing attracted the attention of London literary editors and he rapidly established himself as one of the most influential critics of his generation.

In 1972 he became The Observer's television critic with a weekly column that soon became famous. His articles appear in publications such as the New Yorker, the New York Times, the Los Angeles Times, the Guardian, Spectator and the Australian Book Review. His books include four volumes of autobiography, literary criticism, television criticism, poetry, travel writing and novels. 'Cultural Amnesia', published in 2007, took 40 years to write. For many years he has had a song writing partnership with Cambridge colleague, Pete Atkins. His ability to express something in a very condensed, devastatingly sharp way leaves the reader laughing out loud.

He has had an equally successful media career, presenting for both BBC and ITV, with shows such as 'Clive James on Television', 'The Clive James Show', 'Saturday Night Clive', 'Postcards From', and 'The Clive James Formula 1 Show'. 'Fame in the Twentieth Century' was broadcast in the UK, Australia and the USA. In 2007 he started a weekly BBC R4 broadcast, 'A Point of View'.

He is a member of the Order of Australia (1992) and received an Honorary Doctorate of Letters from Sydney University (1999). In 2003 he was awarded the Philip Hodgins Memorial Medal for his poetry. In 2006 he was awarded an Honorary Doctorate of Letters from the University of East Anglia, and was elected an Honorary Fellow of the Australian Academy of the Humanities. In 2008 he was awarded the George Orwell Special Prize for a lifetime achievement in journalism and broadcasting.

He has learned German, French, Spanish, Italian, Russian and Japanese in order to read works in the original. Despite joking that he barely knows how to turn a computer on he is currently concentrating on his website www.clivejames.com which "gets bigger by the month but ... takes up no room whatsoever". It contains a vast archive of written work, including other authors, art and numerous audio and video interviews.

He spends weekdays at his flat in a converted warehouse in London (complete with dance floor where he can tango) and weekends with his family in Cambridge. He is married to the scholar Prue Shaw and they have two daughters. Loving the limelight and delighting in performing, he also relishes solitude. As a writer who performs he has said that his poetry means the most to him, "a poem will be the last thing I write when I fall off the twig".

Lesley Lawson
'Twiggy'

In 1967 a New Yorker saw Twiggy on her first visit to the US and quipped "She'll last a couple of weeks". Such is Twiggy's beauty and talent that 40 years later she is still an international fashion icon, gracing the front cover of 'Vogue', as well as being an award winning actress and singer.

Born Lesley Hornby in Neasden, London on 19 September 1949, her father was a shopfitter. For pocket money Twiggy had a Saturday job in a hairdressers where she dated a colleague's brother, Justin de Villeneuve. Knowing she wanted to be a model, he engineered an introduction to a fashion editor who, although doubting she was big enough, suggested she get some photos taken. Twiggy spent hours making up her enormous doe-shaped eyes complete with 'Twiggies' (painted on lashes) but her hair was a mess. She was sent to fashionable hairdresser Leonard, who asked Barry Lategan to check if she was photogenic.

Barry's heart sank when he saw her "… there wasn't anything especially outstanding. She was a contradiction to the models of the day." Taking another day off school she went back to Leonard's and after hours of cutting and colouring returned to Barry "She appeared with this short hair cut which was an extraordinary transformation … she sat in front of the camera and it was dazzling." Leonard hung the pictures on the wall of his salon. Twiggy went back to school.

A fashion journalist came in, saw the pictures and asked to meet Twiggy. At this stage Twiggy didn't know what an interview was but was told there'd be a story about her in the Daily Express. Her Dad bought the paper for weeks until a double page spread appeared - 'The Face of 66'. Twiggy had become a star and, aged 16, the world's first supermodel. In 1967 she recorded an album, 'Beautiful Dreams', which won a silver disc and in 1969 became the youngest person ever to appear on 'This is Your Life'.

Ken Russell had seen Twiggy's pictures in Vogue. When he decided to make a film version of 'The Boyfriend' he was adamant he wanted Twiggy in it and sent her off to learn singing and tap (it still keeps her fit). Wanting to discuss the film Russell decided to take her on a day trip to Brighton returning on the Brighton Belle which in those days did a wonderful dinner. However, Twiggy's hand got caught in a chocolate vending machine on the station platform and Ken could only watch the train (and dinner) leave without him as he waited hours for a crowbar to free Twiggy. When the film was released in 1971 Twiggy won two Golden Globes.

Career highlights include a Tony nomination for 'My One And Only', which took Broadway by storm, a TV show 'Twiggy's People' and co-producing and starring in 'If Love Were All'. In 2005 she became a judge on 'America's Next Top Model', and returned to modelling with a hugely successful campaign for M&S. She has her own ranges of clothing and bed linen.

She met her first husband, Michael Witney, co-starring in a thriller 'W'. They married in 1977 and had a daughter, Carly, "the best production of my life"; in 1983 Witney died. Some time later Twiggy went for dinner with Robert Powell and his wife who at the last minute also invited actor Leigh Lawson. Powell recalls Twiggy and Leigh falling in love that night; they married in 1988.

She has sung with Bing Crosby, danced with Noel Coward, received fan mail from Laurence Olivier, her photograph is in a space time capsule and there was a Twiggy Barbie doll; she remains utterly natural. A picture taken in 2000 shows her with Kate Moss, 20 years her junior, but both projecting the same, timeless beauty. As Ken Russell said "Whatever age she is that seems to be the perfect age for Twiggy at that moment."

Jeremy Paxman
'Paxo – A Brand of Stuffing'

He was born in Leeds on 11 May 1950, and educated at Malvern College. He read English at St Catharine's College, Cambridge where he edited the student newspaper, 'Varsity'.

Starting his career in local radio he went on to Northern Ireland as a reporter for the BBC during the Troubles. He returned to work on the 'Tonight' programme, and then 'Panorama' reporting from the Middle East, Africa and Central America. He worked on the 'Six O'clock News' and 'Breakfast Time' until, in 1989, he became presenter of 'Newsnight' making a name for himself as a tough and unrelenting interviewer. He can be intimidating, scary and often his interviews become heated, but they are renowned, with interviewees including Tony Blair, Martin McGuinness, George Galloway, Michael Howard and Cecil Parkinson (whom he memorably asked on the night of New Labour's 1997 landslide victory, "You're director of a fertilizer company. How deep is the mess you're in?").

When asked by Michael Parkinson if he ever felt bad about his interview technique he replied "I have quite often thought… at 3 o'clock in the morning… Oh God I really was a bit rough on… whoever, and it troubles me because in the end they have legitimacy and I don't. They're elected, I'm not." He added that this wasn't the case with Michael Howard when he asked him the same question 14 times and still didn't get an answer, revealing that the reason he kept asking the question was because he had to prolong the interview due to technical problems, and couldn't think of anything else to say.

In 2006 he took part in 'Who Do You Think You Are?' tracing part of his family back to Scotland and finding that his ancestors had been poverty stricken. The public saw a different side to the usually hard edged Paxman when he cried during filming.

Other television work includes chairing 'University Challenge'. His puppet made regular appearances on the satirical show 'Spitting Image' and a warmer, self-deprecating side was revealed when he commented, "I was …. watching Spitting Image which I thought was terribly funny, and then this new character appeared and he spoke in this very odd voice and he was sort of angular and had a large hooter, and I thought who's this supposed to be? A terrible, terrible moment."

He has received Honorary degrees from the Universities of Leeds and Bradford (1999). In 2000 he was made an Honorary Fellow at St Catharine's College, Cambridge and a Fellow by Special Election of St Edmund Hall, Oxford. His awards include the Royal Television Society's Award for International Current Affairs (1985) and Interview/Presenter of the Year (1997, 1998, 2001 and 2008). In 1996 and 1999 he won the Richard Dimbleby Award.

A keen fly fisherman he wrote 'Fish, Fishing and the Meaning of Life'; other works include books on politics, the English and the Royal Family. A republican until he wrote 'On Royalty' when research changed his mind, saying there is "no justification for this institution in the 21st century" but it is "preferable to the alternatives".

His charitable interests include homelessness, mental health and education.

His partner is Elizabeth Ann Clough; they have a son and two daughters.

Finally, this hardened interviewer has revealed that he did chicken out of one opportunity: "There's something about this diminutive little old lady that suddenly had me really poleaxed with anxiety. I just thought 'No, I don't want to do this at all. I ran away' ". The scary lady? The Queen.

Libby Purves OBE
'Broadcaster, Journalist and Author'

She was born on 2 February 1950 in London, the only daughter in a family of four. Her father was a diplomat which meant she attended various foreign schools; including a French convent where she learned French (invaluable for finding out what had really gone on at EU summits when Press Secretary Bernard Ingham was parsimonious with information at press conferences, in stark contrast to French journalists' briefings).

She won a scholarship to St Anne's College, Oxford, graduating with a first class degree in English Language and Literature, and was elected Librarian of the Union. In her finals year she worked for Radio Oxford as a student volunteer.

From her earliest years she was fascinated by radios and, aged 7, saved pocket money to buy a DIY transistor kit. It took a week to build and finally produced, to her joy, a crackle and then a tiny thread of Morse.

She trained to work on the technical side of broadcasting, joining the BBC as a trainee Programme Operations Assistant. Her first posting was the World Service, where she worked for a year before rejoining Radio Oxford as Station Assistant; the work entailed announcing, interviewing, presenting and producing, plus being a DJ. In 1974 she joined Radio 4's 'Today' programme as Trainee Producer, before returning to Radio Oxford to present and report.

She has always done things her way and a year later left the BBC to freelance, a move she has never regretted, "I am not a Human Resource! I am Libby Purves Limited, and only as good as my last tape!" She rejoined 'Today' as a presenter (the youngest ever, and first female) but on her own terms, insisting on six weeks off to sail across the Atlantic, two months into the job. She continued to host 'Today' until 1981, and broadcast the first ever live programme in China, from Beijing.

She has hosted a TV show, 'Choices', and was briefly Editor of 'Tatler'. In 1983 she became presenter of 'Midweek' on Radio 4 where she also presented 'The Learning Curve'. Not bad for someone who was told her voice was not suitable for a career as a broadcaster.

She is a columnist for The Times where her fiercely independent articles go straight to the heart of the questions of the day. As she has said "Ask questions beginning with "why?"" at least once a day. Point out that, even if the emperor does have clothes, they're on inside out."

She married Paul Heiney in 1980 (despite working as rivals and being fed misinformation about each other by their boss). They have two children, Rose, and Nicholas who died in 2006, aged 23. She has published a collection of his writings, 'The Silence at the Song's End', some of which have been set to music by Joseph Phibbs.

Apart from radio and writing her passions include opera and sailing. She and her husband sailed round Britain with the children, then aged 3 and 5, in a 38' cutter ('One Summer's Grace'). Her descriptions of sailing when everything is going right are a delight, making one long to purchase a yacht, obtain a Master's Certificate and set sail, eg, "The next watch … was a rare delight, a rare reminder of why we spend so much effort and money on going sailing … I was alone; Lyme Bay lay broad and dark around me with ships' lights to avoid and roguish waves … ; that was my task, but the boat herself was my private joy: a perfect thing gracing a perfect night, carrying my sleeping family; a world complete."

She has written books on childcare and family life, novels and memoirs. In 1999 she was appointed OBE for services to journalism, and named Columnist of the Year. She is a Patron of the Professional Cartoonists Organisation.

BBC

Jeremy Vine
'Clean Cut Journalist, Broadcaster & TV Presenter'

The eldest of three children he was born on 17 May 1965 in Epsom, Surrey. His brother is the comedian, Tim Vine, and his sister the artist and actress, Sonya Vine. His first taste of a radio career came aged 12 when he appeared on Kenny Everett's Young DJ slot at Capital Radio. Unbelievably, as a teenager, he was a punk rocker, playing drums in 'The Flared Generation'. The band's attempts to break into the charts were dashed when their debut vinyl came off the presses oval instead of round.

Educated at Epsom College he went on to read English Literature at Durham University. Whilst there he contacted Metro Radio in Newcastle and was given the graveyard 2am – 5am slot (presumably ideal for a student). After leaving Durham he worked for the Coventry Evening Telegraph and a year later joined the BBC on its prestigious news trainee programme. John Birt joined on the same day, but whilst Birt went on to become Director General, complete with knighthood, it is said that Jeremy still yearns to be recognised by the BBC's car park staff.

His BBC career has been a classic fast track one, starting as a reporter on Radio 4's 'Today' programme where reports included an interview with a redundant ballistics missile expert in Siberia, mafia scams in southern Italy and sheep racing in Dorset. Next came work as a lobby correspondent, and then a posting to Johannesburg as Africa Correspondent. He covered elections in Algeria, Aids in Mali, and events in Zimbabwe, including one of Robert Mugabe's last ever interviews with the BBC. He also reported on wars in Sudan, Angola and Ethiopia and events in numerous other African nations. In an extraordinary film that won the Silver Nymph at Monte Carlo, he revealed police brutality in Johannesburg resulting in the suspension of 22 police officers, two of whom were later convicted.

Then came a chance as stand-in presenter on BBC2's 'Newsnight' graduating to full-time presenter in 1999 – he was the presenter on 9/11. He is philosophical about the "mini-me" gibe from the main presenter, Jeremy Paxman, and since he believes that too hostile an approach to politicians produces gridlock and brings the media into disrepute 'Newsnight' was probably never going to be the right vehicle for him. However, he has had his run ins with politicians, notably during the 2001 general election when he toured the UK in a 1970s VW camper van spray painted with Newsnight's logo - Peter Mandelson famously stormed out of it when asked if he thought Gordon Brown was having a perfect election campaign. Previously John Major had told him "You're a very impatient boy" when he asked a question out of turn.

In 2003 he launched BBC1's 'The Politics Show', and, amidst considerable controversy, took over the BBC R2 lunchtime slot from Jimmy Young with the very successful 'The Jeremy Vine Show'. In 2007 he launched a re-vamped 'Panorama' and in 2008 took over 'Points of View' from Terry Wogan. Since 2008 he has co-hosted a quiz show 'Eggheads'.

In 1996 he won an Amnesty International Radio Award for a report about a former child soldier, Civilian, he met in Sierra Leone. In 2005 he won the best speech broadcaster award at the Sony Radio Academy Awards.

In 2002 he married Rachel Schofield and they have two daughters. His interests include Chelsea FC, Hitchcock films and WH Auden's poems. He also writes poetry and has a strong Christian faith, although no longer evangelical. For Children in Need he appeared as Frank-N-Furter complete with fishnet stockings and suspenders.

For him the unexpected replies are the best part of journalism, citing an interview with an Italian police spokeswoman whom he was asking about crime in Naples and whether it was completely out of control – her answer – "No, it is in the control of four families."

How to Buy

PEOPLE OF THE DAY   **ISBN 978-0-9548110-0-3**

This first volume examines the lives of 51 individuals, ranging from the dyslexic entrepreneur Richard Branson, to the chosen one of the Tibetan people, the Dalai Lama. From the politically correct ... to the less so.

PEOPLE OF THE DAY 2   **ISBN 978-0-9548110-1-1**

This second volume returns with 52 caricatures from across a wide spectrum; from Basil Fawlty himself, Mr John Cleese, to the man who "devoted his life to music", Luciano Pavarotti.

PEOPLE OF THE DAY 3   **ISBN 978-0-9548110-2-0**

This third volume features a further 52 caricatures of the rich and famous including the likes of HRH The Princess Royal, Boris Johnson, Sir Stuart Rose, Gary Lineker, Brian Blessed, Ringo Starr and Sir David Attenborough.

PEOPLE OF THE DAY 4   **ISBN 978-0-9548110-3-7**

The fourth volume of this ever more popular series of books profiles the likes of Joanna Lumley, Sir Ranulph Fiennes, President Barack Obama, Dame Vivienne Westwood and Johnny Depp.

Available to buy through

Waterstone's, WH Smith, Amazon, Tesco and all high street bookshops

You can purchase any of the People of the Day books directly from the author on line at:

www.peopleoftheday.com

Or by completing the order form
SEE OVER FOR ORDER FORM

LIMITED EDITION CARICATURE PRINTS

Limited edition prints of all the caricatures featured in the books are available to purchase exclusively from:

www.peopleoftheday.com

Digitally printed and presented on 300gsm high quality silk finished paper, 297mm x 420mm.
Each print is accompanied by a copy of the individual profile.

To view the extensive caricature gallery and order your limited edition prints visit:

www.peopleoftheday.com

Please contact us with any enquiries either by telephone +44 (0)1276 859483 or email

info@peopleoftheday.co.uk.

Order Form

Please send completed forms, along with payment, to:

ORDERS
People of the Day Limited
Sunnymede, New England Hill
West End, Woking
Surrey GU24 9PY

Cheques or postal orders should be made payable to **'People of the Day Limited'**. **PLEASE DO NOT SEND CASH.** Goods will be despatched via second class mail on receipt of payment. Please allow 7 to 10 days for delivery. Confirmation of order and despatch by email only.

Email Address ____

Please tick here if you do not wish to receive any special offers or discounts available. ☐
Please tick here if you do not wish to be contacted by us regarding other products. ☐

BILLING ADDRESS

Name: ____

Address: ____

____

Post code: ____

DELIVERY ADDRESS (if different from above)

Name: ____

Address: ____

____

Post code: ____

Number of books required: Volume 1 _______   Volume 2 _______
Volume 3 _______   Volume 4 _______

I enclose total amount of £ ____
(please include appropriate postal charge as stated below.)

Postage and Packing Charges

UK	£1.50 for the first book	50p for each additional book purchased
Europe (airmail)	£3.00 for the first book	£2.00 for each additional book purchased
Elsewhere (airmail)	£6.00 for the first book	£4.00 for each additional book purchased

For any queries please telephone People of the Day Limited on **+44 (0)1276 859483**
or email **info@peopleoftheday.co.uk.**

Prices and availability are subject to change without notice.
